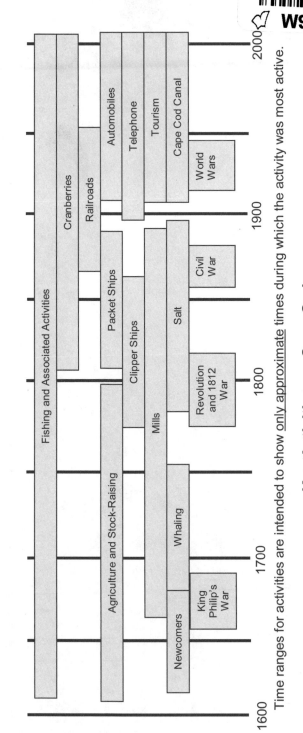

Key Activities on Cape Cod

Timeline courtesy of Edward Weissberger

Time ranges for activities are intended to show only approximate times during which the activity was most active.

Reflections Of Cape Cod
Stories Of The People, Towns and Times

by Ruth M. Weissberger

Green Teal Publishing

16 Green Teal Way
Yarmouth Port, MA 02675

Editing and Imaging by Edward Weissberger

Printed in the United States of America by Phoenix Color Corp.
540 Western Maryland Parkway
Hagerstown, MA 21740

Library of Congress Cataloging-in-Publication Data
Weissberger, Ruth M.
Reflections of Cape Cod
Stories of The People, Towns and Times
Ruth M. Weissberger. – 1st ed.

Includes Index
ISBN 0-9728582-0-2

Dedication

For my husband Ted, whose patience, understanding and guidance fills my world with the true meaning of love.

In memory of Kenneth and Esther Mackall, who continue to be my inspiration.

REFLECTIONS OF CAPE COD

Table of Contents

Table of Images

Acknowledgements

I would like to thank the many people who gave their support to this project. Without the help of my husband, Dr. Edward Weissberger, *Reflections of Cape Cod* could not have been completed. His tireless work with editing and imaging not only took skill but patience as well. My brothers, Dr. Richard Delmonico and Dr. Ronald Delmonico, were a constant source of encouragement throughout this endeavor and kept me going when I felt truly bogged down.

Laurel Gabel, a noted author on cemeteries, gravestones and gravestone carvers, helped enormously regarding my research in a field that can be very confusing. Duncan Oliver, a noted author of Cape Cod history, helped with historical accuracy. I was also very fortunate to have Bill Barnes of *The Register* offer help with editing suggestions and research material. *The Register* helped tremendously by giving permission for use of their photographs.

And of course, my children, Mark and Maria, were always ready to listen when I needed an understanding ear.

My sincere thanks and appreciation to you all.

Preface

After falling in love with Cape Cod and eventually retiring to Yarmouth Port, I became involved with the history that brought this land to what it is today. I am not the only one to fall in love with the Cape and become involved with its evolution. People do not need to be here long before questions regarding whaling, leaders in local towns, and economic growth become more than mere curiosity. As with all research, one question leads to another. Eventually I found that I was telling the story of Cape Cod's history to groups who were also interested in this fascinating land. Before long, the stories of Cape Cod's people, towns and times grew into this work. It became clear to me that we are indeed a reflection of this remarkable land and that it takes a certain kind of person to live here.

This book is my gift to all who fall in love with Cape Cod and want to know more about how such an ever changing land attracted and held people who are as changing as the land on which they live.

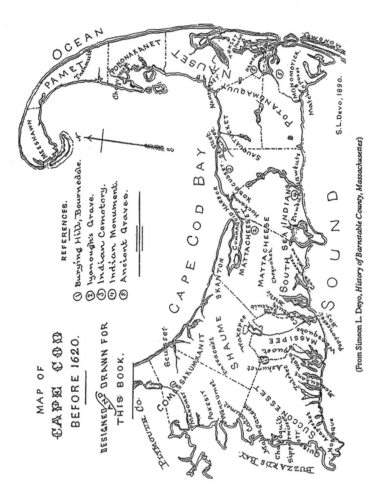

Cape Cod Before 1620
From Simeon L. Deyo, History of Barnstable County, Massachusetts

Reflections Of Cape Cod
Stories Of The People, Towns and Times

INTRODUCTION

The purpose of this book is to share the history of Cape Cod. It is a story of people and their land. It is a story of struggle, survival and growth. But most important, it is a story of how free people living in a democratic, capitalistic society are able to change the way they live in response to external and internal changes. The people who chose to live here have had the character, strength and freedom to adapt to changes and to make alterations to improve the society in which they lived. This is a story of people improving their lives, independent of government direction, and as such is illustrative of how our country has prospered.

The economy of the Cape is impacted by events occurring in the world. These events also emotionally impact Cape Cod residents. From the late 1600s, as whaling became a major industry, to the present day when tourism leads the economy, Cape Cod and its people have dealt with changing tides of world events. Storms, wars, changing industry and even changes in the land itself have carved the character of Cape Codders and have given them the world in which they find themselves today.

While this history draws on examples from Yarmouth and the mid-Cape region, its real emphasis is on how people adapted to changes. As such, it is a history of all of Cape Cod and its people.

CHAPTER 1:
MAKING A LIVING

Whaling

Nature is the main force that marks Cape Cod as unique, both in the ever changing land and in the way those who choose to live on this land cope with changes. When the newcomers arrived in the 1600s, they set about making their living through agriculture, stock-raising and fishing. Just getting by was hard work but there were occasional luxuries, as when a whale washed up onto shore. The tale of the whale is fascinating, as whaling progressed from harvesting beached whales, to hunting them from small boats, to worldwide, multi-year hunting trips and eventually to observing whales swimming about a sight-seeing boat.

Cape Cod was made famous by the whaling skill of its people. In early times, whales abounded in Cape Cod waters and often became stranded on the Cape's shores. Sometimes a whole pod stranded, and farmers left their fields and rushed to the beach to tend to the profits that could be made from this gift from the sea. These early *whalers* never embarked on boats. The bounty came to them. They simply went to the beach where the whales stranded, stripped the blubber and rendered it into oil which was used primarily for lighting.

Whale Oil Lamps
Photo courtesy of Edward Weissberger

A noted historian wrote:

> "The townspeople looked upon whaling as a lark, particularly since the profits were immediate: and before long some began to wish that whales would come ashore often enough to provide steady work at trying them out. At this point the seed was sown that was to turn the Cape Codders into whalemen."[1]

Drift whales, or stranded whales, were shared among the people, with the minister, the church and the school of the town in which the whales had stranded. Shore whaling brought such profits that men set up outer beach houses as watch sites. It took a lot of wood to keep these houses warm and the wood burned contributed to the stripping of the Cape's forests.

Soon there were disagreements over which town owned a beached whale. Lively discussions developed over where a large whale, or pod of smaller pilot whales, called *blackfish*, had beached and which town had claim. Before the town of Sandwich was twenty years old it had already promulgated rules and regulations concerning drift whales.

Profits from shore whaling were substantial. In 1687, two hundred tons of whale oil were exported to England. Boiled and refined, it lubricated delicate machinery. Whale blubber was rendered and the resulting oil used in the tanning process and for lighting.

Blackfish are small whales, more accurately large dolphins, that swim in large pods and frequently enter Cape Cod Bay. They are now called *pilot whales* as they swim in large groups with one member acting as the leader or pilot. Pilot whales range in length from six to twenty feet, occasionally longer. More than one hundred pilot whales will sometimes strand on a beach at one time.

People soon realized that they could hunt whales on Cape Cod Bay and passive shore whaling evolved into active whaling with men working from small boats. Whale watches were established at specific locations and when whales were sighted, boats were launched in pursuit. Areas for sighting whales were called *whaling grounds* or reservations -- one such reservation was established on the north shore in the northwestern part of the town we now know as Dennis.

Soon, Cape Cod men achieved fame for their ability to hunt and kill whales. During the 1690s, residents of Nantucket Island asked Ichabod Paddock of Yarmouth to come and teach them the skills needed to kill whales from small boats and to extract cherished whale oil.

As more and more men left their farms to pursue whales, the whale population declined and became insufficient to support a whaling industry working only in the shallow waters of Cape Cod Bay. This greatly affected the people of Cape Cod's towns.

"In 1739, only about half a dozen whales were taken in Provincetown waters, and a number of families decided to move away. Ten years later, the citizens of Yarmouth were so impoverished by the failure of the whale-fishery that they were barely able to give the minister an increase in salary they had promised him. Wellfleet, during the years preceding the Revolution, devoted almost her entire energy to whaling. Nearly every man in town was a whaleman, and the result of thus putting all the eggs in one basket was that the declaration of war in 1775 and the immediate blockading of the Cape ports utterly prostrated the town. The citizens could not pay the Provincial tax and, in a petition to the General Court for exemption, they declared that nine tenths of the townsmen had been engaged in whaling and were now left with no source of income."[2]

If whaling were to continue as a means of making a living, whalers had no choice but to pursue whales in deeper waters. Off-shore whaling was a dangerous business for both men and ships and potential losses were substantial. In addition, shore whalers did not have sufficient capital to invest in boats and equipment needed to work in deep water nor were there deep water harbors on Cape Cod necessary to accommodate large, ocean-going vessels.

As always, there were a few men who made the best of a difficult situation; Colonel Elisha Doane was one of these men. As whalers went farther and farther out to sea, he financed voyages and reaped a good share of the profits. This was certainly better than taking on the danger of going to sea himself. Colonel Doane was so successful in this and other businesses that he died a very wealthy man.

Yarmouth's *whaling grounds* had been set aside by and were owned by the town for the purpose of shore whaling. When shore whaling lost its commercial value, Yarmouth's citizens voted at town meeting to sell that land. Whaling grounds then remained as private property until later centuries when many areas were re-purchased as public beaches and conservation lands.

As is often the case today, people of those times did not recognize that some of the things they did were harmful to the land and thereby to themselves as well. Harvesting lumber for fishing vessels, for homes and fireplaces as well as the clearing of land for agriculture, stripped the forests. Farmers failed to replenish nutrients depleted from the soil and land became less and less productive. Whales were taken in such quantity that their population decreased and whaling as a way of living was forced to undergo dramatic changes.

Even though the whale population was decreasing, land was becoming less fertile and forests were disappearing, the Cape's economy was in fact growing. In the mid-1600s, farms produced Indian corn, vegetables and fruit. A good crop of corn was as good as money because it could be used in trade, in payment for needed manufactured items or to pay one's taxes. There was fish and game to eat and livestock in the field and, of course, *home brew*. Salaries and bills were often paid with such items of trade, which were as welcome as silver. Often the minister was paid with firewood and it has been said that

Squire Doane, Colonel Doane's son, often partially paid workers with rum.

Salt

The salt industry was critical to the fishing trade. Before refrigeration, salt was key to preserving fish for shipment to distant dining rooms. March through October were salt making months and the saltworks of South Yarmouth, which supplied many with employment, was quite an operation. In addition to evaporation ponds, windmills which drove pumps lined both the north and south shores of Yarmouth.

Saltworks at Bass River
Notice Pumping Windmill on the Right
Photo courtesy of Alex & Audrey Todd

Mr. John Sears, called Sleepy John, began salt production in 1776 after experimenting with an evaporation process. Dennis Freeman described Sears' operation:

"... this ingenious seaman constructed a vat a hundred feet long and ten feet wide. Rafters were fixed over it, and shutters were contrived to move up and down, that the vat might be covered when it rained and exposed to the heat of the sun in fair weather. By this simple invention the rain was excluded, the water in the vat was gradually exhaled, and at length, to his inexpressible joy, Captain Sears perceived the salt beginning to crystallize. His works, however, were leaky, and he had such bad success in his operations the first year that he was unable to obtain more than eight bushels of salt. He was exposed besides to the ridicule of his neighbors, who scoffed at his invention, styling it Sears's Folly."[3]

Necessity being the mother of invention, Sears introduced many process improvements, including using pumps rather than hand carried buckets to bring saltwater to evaporation vats. Each improvement brought improved salt production. Eventually, others invented mechanical devices to move the large heavy vat covers so that the covers did not have to be moved by hand. These covers prevented rain from re-filling evaporation tanks. The many improvements made by others were reassigned to Sleepy John who then received a patent on his saltworks in 1799.

One by-product of salt production was magnesia which was used in the production of milk of magnesia. Another was Glaubers salt, which tanners used to keep hides soft.[a]

In 1830, there were eighteen saltworks along Yarmouth's northern shore. More, however, were along the shore of South Yarmouth. In 1837, 365,200 bushels of salt were produced in Yarmouth alone and Dennis produced an additional 52,000 bushels.

---

[a] Magnesia is magnesium oxide and Glaubers salt is a hydrated form of sodium sulfate.

Model of Pumping Windmill
Pumping windmills delivered saltwater to evaporation vats.
Model owned by the Historical Society of Old Yarmouth
Photo courtesy of Edward Weissberger

Evaporation Vats with Sliding Covers
Note how large the vats are by comparison to the men
Photo courtesy of Stanley Snow

Material handling was an enormous task. Approximately 350 gallons of sea water were required to produce just one bushel of salt. Each town had many establishments producing salt; Yarmouth had 52 saltworks, Dennis had 114, and Brewster had 60. In one year alone, the thirteen towns of Cape Cod produced over twenty-six thousand tons of salt. Clearly, this was a major industry in the 1800s.

Most of the salt was consumed by the thriving fishing industry which needed salt to preserve the catches. One vessel alone could consume about 700 bushels a year. As the fishing industry grew, the salt industry grew with it. Salt was also used in international commerce as trade for rum and sugar in the West Indies.

Salt manufacturing on Cape Cod was in part a consequence of the American Revolution. During the war, the British blockade put a stop to salt importing, allowing John Sears to sell salt from his newly developed saltworks at inflated wartime prices. Salt manufacturing was also strongly influenced by the War of 1812, which residents of Cape Cod and the Islands considered a repeat of the Revolution, because of its deleterious impact on trade.

Paul Schneider wrote:

"... opposition on Cape Cod and the Islands to 'Mr. Madison's War' and the resulting disruption of trade was even more widespread than loyalism had been in the Revolution. Although the English policy of impressing American sailors into their navy - the nominal reason for the hostilities - was universally hated on Cape Cod and the Islands, only Sandwich, Barnstable, Falmouth, and Orleans were openly in favor of war. On the Vineyard, too, opinion was decidedly mixed. And once again,

Nantucket attempted to broker a separate deal for herself, going so far as to promise the English not to pay taxes to the United States government. As a result, two British admirals, one of them named Coffin, went to England's infamous Dartmoor Prison and singled out the Nantucket sailors to inform them that they would soon be released. But as it had a generation before, the Nation of Nantucket wound up just as destitute as her neighbors by war's end. Once again, dozens of families left the Cape and Islands for good."[4]

By the 1870s, the price of salt had begun to decline. Salt deposits were found in the west and salt mining was far less costly than evaporative production. In addition, conservation issues resulting from a shortage of trees were also significant -- lumber had become too scarce to be cost effectively used to build salt vats.

Fishing

Fishing has always been a way of life on Cape Cod. Today, as in earlier times, the excitement of the catch is exhilarating and shared fishing stories are the glue of friendship. Shore fishing from piers and beaches along Cape Cod Bay, Nantucket Sound and the Atlantic Ocean were and remain sources of food, relaxation and friendship. Families and friends try their luck and test their skills. When strolling a beach one often sees tubes dug into the sand to hold fishing poles, with fishermen resting alongside. Other fishermen cast into the surf, just as they did in past years.

Early on, Monomoy island was a particularly attractive site for shore fishing. But as it was with whaling, people soon recognized that there were more fish to be had out to sea and soon fishing schooners gathered in hopes of a larger catch.

Another type of fishing is weir fishing. Weir poles are still seen off shore, especially on the south side, where they serve a role in the modern fishing industry. From the 1830s to the 1880s, weir fishing played a much bigger role in Cape Cod's fishing economy than it does today.

Weirs work in an interesting way. Weir nets stretch from pole to pole and trap fish that swim among them. The fish then follow the leader line of nets through a maze, eventually swimming into an area where they can see fish on the other side of the net. Once in, they cannot escape the maze of netting around and under them.

On the south side, fishing boats still go to the weirs where fishermen grab the center of the nets and draw them, along with the trapped fish, into their boat. It's hard, heavy work and a great deal of strength is need for this task.

On the north side, trap weirs were used, a system that did not require boats. Men spread nets over the gently sloping flats at low tide, and when the fish came in with the rising tide, they closed the nets about the fish by pulling the nets toward shore using horse drawn carts. Large wheels allowed the carts to work in water and on soft sand. Once the horses had drawn the fish into an area where they were impounded, the fish were shoveled into the cart. Horses then pulled the cart back to shore. This type of weir fishing was not easy both because there are channels through the flats making skillful maneuvering of horse drawn carts difficult and because the work of shoveling fish into carts was a back breaking task.

The fishing industry on Cape Cod has had its ups and downs throughout the years. At the start of the American revolution, Plymouth and Chatham had large fishing fleets, Chatham's fleet being comprised of 27 cod vessels. By the war's end in 1783, only five remained.

By 1789, fishing fleets had expanded as the government paid a bounty on exported cod. During the 1800s, the fishing industry improved with abundant schools of cod, mackerel and herring running off the shores of Plymouth and from 1826 to about 1863, fishing fleets were large. Wellfleet had a fleet of seventy-five schooners and an active oyster business. Dennis, Chatham and Harwich fished for mackerel. However, Chatham's cod fleet had declined as silting made access to the harbor difficult.

By the late 1800s, commercial fishing from Cape Cod had once again declined, this time due to new, expanded, more efficient alternative fisheries. New transportation technology, primarily railroads, dramatically enhanced both the speed with which goods could be moved and the quantity of goods that could be moved. At first this aided New England's fishing industry by expediting transport to new and established markets alike. But soon, increased competition took its toll as the Great Lakes developed lucrative fisheries.

New Technology And Fishing

New technology impacted who was able to fish. With the introduction of seines, physical strength became paramount and only men, as opposed to young boys, could be employed. Consequently, boys needing employment had to look elsewhere.

Young men interested in year-round work as an improvement over seasonal fishing, moved inland away from Cape Cod. Further, because fishing on the open sea is a dangerous business, many women preferred not to marry fishermen in fear of being widowed. This social fact also drove many away from a life at sea.

In 1905, John R. Neal, a Boston fish dealer, built an *otter trawler* and named it *The Spray*. The term now used for an *otter trawler* is *draggerboat*. Prior to this invention, most fishing had been line fishing. Taking its name from Neal's boat, spray fishing was accomplished by dragging large nets along the bottom of the sea, scooping up anything in their paths. Within ten years, John Neal was the largest fish producer in New England.

Dragging has always been a controversial fishing method, the problem being that immature baby cod and haddock are taken along with mature, large fish. Also, the quantity of fish taken at one time can be huge which dramatically reduces the food supply for larger fish. Food for bottom feeders is also taken as nets scrape along the bottom. Tons of dead small fish and potential food are dumped and found floating on the surface, wasted. Some people have blamed spray fishing for the decline in fish populations that presently impacts the fishing industry.

Cape Cod took its name from the codfish that, along with herring, abounded in its waters and served as a staple of its fishing industry. Even today, people go to see herring running in spring and still scoop them up, filling their nets.

The great fishing days of Cape Cod are a thing of the past. Today, people fish for pleasure and some struggle to make a living from the sea. The waters do not abound with fish as they did in early days and there is much discussion of conservation and limits. Fishermen's lives have become increasingly difficult.

The Cape Cod Cranberry

Native Americans and early European settlers ate cranberries that grew wild like blueberries and other fruits. Europeans called them *crane berry* because the delicate vine to which the berry is attached reminded them of a crane's neck.

Producing a very tart fruit, cranberry vines grow naturally in bogs but in colonial times the fruit did not spark the imagination of many people. Indeed, bogs in which they grew were considered worthless land. However, in 1816, Henry Hall, a farmer in Dennis, noticed that cranberry vines growing in bogs into which sand had blown produced a better crop than vines growing without addition of fresh sand. Cape Cod's sandy soil and strong winds worked together to enhance natural cranberry production.

Hall experimented with the amount of sand needed to increase cranberry production and as cranberries became more available from natural bogs to which sand had been added, demand for these nutritious berries increased. Harwich, which had many bogs, became the site of a thriving industry.

During the early 1800s, cranberries, with their high vitamin C content, were carried on board ships to help prevent scurvy. In 1847, the first commercial cranberry bog was planted and soon many planters began clearing their bogs and cultivating the berry.

Farmers continued experimenting to increase the yield, size and flavor of cranberries. Three years after planting, a bog begins to produce berries and in the 1800s a large bog could support a family. Cranberry production requires a great deal of work and a well cared for bog can produce cranberries indefinitely. Bogs planted in the 1800s are still in operation today, well over one hundred years after they began production.

Harwich Cranberry Bog
Photo courtesy of Edward Weissberger

As with all products, quality control is essential in ensuring a profitable cranberry harvest. The way to test if a cranberry is of high quality is to drop it onto a hard floor. It does sound crazy, but the truth is that a good cranberry will bounce as high as four inches and this is still how cranberries are tested within the cranberry industry. Berries are graded according to how high they bounce. Another interesting trait of this unique fruit is that it floats, a much appreciated characteristic as it allows wet harvesting.

Cranberry Harvesting

There are two methods by which cranberries are harvested on Cape Cod, wet harvesting and dry harvesting. Before the invention of modern mechanical harvesting equipment, wet harvesting had the advantage of being quick and easy. As bogs are flooded, ripe berries float from their vines and then are taken from the bog. Because they become water saturated as a consequence of the harvesting process, these berries are not suitable for dry packaging and are used for drinks. Dry picked berries are the ones found in packages of fresh fruit so popular at Thanksgiving dinners.

In the early and middle 1800s, prior to the development of wet harvesting, dry berries were picked by hand. As with many harvests, children were excused from school to participate in harvesting. Necessity proved the mother of invention and the cranberry scoop was introduced to increase productivity.

Wooden Cranberry Scoop
From the collection of the Historical Society of Old Yarmouth
Photo courtesy of Edward Weissberger

Wooden cranberry scoops have fork-like tines extending from something akin to an open bucket. The scoop is held by a handle and worked across the vines as the picker crawls on his or her knees through the bog. Small scoops were used to get close to the edge of the bog so that no berries were wasted.

Typically, a full scoop could hold six quarts of berries and a single thrust into the vines would produce about four quarts. A skilled person could pick a bushel of berries in five minutes. Use of scoops also enhanced production by raising the vines. This aided vine growth thus providing a better crop during the next season.

With the scoop, it became uneconomical to harvest missed berries, which were left in the bog. Hand picking damaged vines as pickers attempted to untangle the vines. Later, a scoop with a rocker bottom made working the bog even easier and this type of scoop was used into the 1950s. Eventually, new mechanized techniques were devised to increase productivity and production.

Small Metal-Tined Cranberry Scoop
Bottom and Top
From the collection of the Historical Society of Old Yarmouth
Photo Courtesy of Edward Weissberger

The Cranberry Industry

On August 14, 1930, the Cape Cod cranberry became an economic boon when three major growers formed the Ocean Spray Cooperative. The Register reported that Marcus Urann of Wareham, an Ocean Spray co-founder, wrote to growers:

> "Work as you must, worry as you will, kill bugs and flow for frost, still your profit depends upon the supply and demand for cranberries. Let us Cape Codders throw out our chest, take pride and every day boost and blow and blow for Ocean Spray brand cranberry sauce. Ten million people will visit Cape Cod this year, and they shall not pass without seeing, feeling, hearing and tasting cranberries."

In 1931, Ocean Spray introduced the cranberry juice drink. Soon cranberry juice was being mixed with other juices, bringing Florida citrus growers into the business. In 1999, *The Register* headed an article on cranberries, *They don't call it a 'Cape Codder' because of the vodka.*

One of the true delights of living on Cape Cod is seeing these beautiful bogs in fall, bright red amongst the green of the landscape. Today, growers of the historical berries are struggling to keep their industry alive. As other parts of the country have developed cranberry production and demand for Cape Cod cranberries has decreased, bogs are being sold or taken out of production. Again, industry shifts and times change.

In the late 1930s, this **cranberry** *bottle stood in Onset where Cape visitors were visually alerted to the booming cranberry industry.*

Postcard courtesy of Noel W. Beyle

Cranberry Cocktail Roadside Stand
Photo courtesy of *The Register*

Mills, Millers and Millwrights

The phrase, *keeping ones nose to the grindstone* made more sense in the 1800s than it does in today's world. Today, stately windmills still stand like majestic giants, set back from the road, telling a story of a lost art and an industry no longer in existence.

Grains, especially corn, ground into flour in the Cape's mills were an important part of the early settlers' diet.

Millers and windmills were central to community life. Millwrights, who built and maintained windmills, were highly skilled craftsmen and were well paid, as were the millers themselves. In addition to being exempt from military duty, millers benefited from not having to pay taxes on their mills and were often given the land next to their mills. Frequently, the miller was paid in corn, an amount known as the miller's *pottle*.

Windmills have been described as half ship and half house as they embody the characteristics of both. Dos Passos and Shay, wrote:

"They were circular or hexagonal and built of heavy oak timbers. Strips of canvas for sails were fastened to the arms. In a forty mile gale you would have a twelve horsepower engine and running them was a difficult, almost nautical, job. Many of the millers were retired seamen."[5]

It is from the windmill that the saying *three sheets to the wind* is derived, for when only three of four sheets (or sails) were set, the windmill would wobble and it looked like someone who had had too much to drink.

Windmills were so cherished and so difficult to build that they were often dismantled and rebuilt at new locations rather than building a new one from scratch at a new location. When reading plaques on historic, refurbished mills today, one can see that most are not located where they originally stood.

Judah Baker Windmill
A *Smock Mill* with conical cap and one dormer
(Wind sails removed for winter)
Built 1791 above Grand Cove, S. Dennis
Moved to Kelly's Pond, Dennis
Moved to Bass River, South Yarmouth, 1866
Restored 1974 and 1999
Photo courtesy of Edward Weissberger

Water powered mills were easier to construct and maintain, but were more restricted in where they could be placed as they depended on a strongly flowing river or stream. Many waterwheel powered mills were constructed along the streams of Yarmouth, Brewster, Barnstable, Bourne, Falmouth, Eastham, Truro and Sandwich.

Millers and mills are now stories from the past, tales of a life and occupation that existed from the 1600s until the late 1800s. The last working mill on Cape Cod was located in Orleans and ceased operation in 1892. The oldest mill in America was the Farris mill, brought to Bass River from Sandwich and then moved again to West Yarmouth by a team of twenty oxen. It was eventually bought by Henry Ford and to this day remains off Cape.

No longer do millers keep their noses to the grindstone where the smell of burning grain would tell them they were grinding too fast.

To the Farris Windmill
by Daniel Wing

Now take thy rest, thou good old mill
From peak of roof to oaken sill;
No more thine arms go circling round,
Thy noisome gears emit no sound.
No more thy vanes point to the breeze,
For now thou take'st thy well-earned ease
While millers known to thee of yore
Have lived their lives and gone before.
Long time ago, thy oaken frame
Out from the native forest came;
Those massive grinders brought from far,
E'en to this day thy pride they are.
That iron shaft made strong to stand

REFLECTIONS OF CAPE COD

Thy weight above, was forged by hand,
For hammers then weren't run by steam.
To work on shaft, or band, or beam.
Then, workers toiled from sun to sun,
Their daily wage was fully won;
They did not quit at three or four
And go right home to work no more.
Thous't done thy duty long and well;
We would today thy praises swell,
For good example thou hast set
Which mortal man should not forget.
Though winds blew high or winds blew low,
Thy steady course did onward go:
With sails adjusted to the breeze
Thy work was always done to please.
Man raised the grain; though made'st it fit
To make the "staff of life" of it.
In this, thou'st nobly done thy part;
So thou, a benefactor art.
The mealy stream no more runs out
Into the trough from wooden spout;
For the grinding has ceased,
The meal does no flow;
Memories only remain
Of those scenes long ago.

Taken from *The Register,* Yarmouth Port, MA.

---

[1] Cape Cod Its People and Their History, Henry C. Kittredge, page 165.
[2] Cape Cod Its People and Their History, Henry C. Kittredge, pages 171, 172.
[3] History of Old Yarmouth, Charles F. Swift, Page 257 (Dennis Freeman, 135-137, *cf.* Thacher: Salt (in bibliography)).
[4] The Enduring Shore, Paul Schneider, Page 229.
[5] Down Cape Cod, Katharine Dos Passos and Edith Shay, page 58.

CHAPTER 2:
RIGS, RAILS AND ROADS

Clipper Ships and Captains

The early to mid-1800s were wonderful times. Business was thriving. There were social activities, church activities and town affairs to attend to. These were times of diversification within industry, political views and religious expression.

The most romantic era of Cape Cod was the days of the sea captains. Captain Asa Eldridge set his long-held record for a North Atlantic crossing aboard the clipper ship *Red Jacket*, going from New York to Liverpool in only thirteen days and one hour. By the 1800s, maritime trade was the Cape's leading industry.

Navigation on the open sea without landmarks as guides was critically important and difficult. Indeed, good navigation was an art in itself. Mary Matthews Bray described her experiences traveling to India from Cape Cod via London aboard her father's ship *National Eagle*.

"The Captain takes the sextant and brings it down to the level of the horizon. When it begins to dip, he looks at his watch, to see how many seconds it is from twelve, and how many seconds variation there is between the present day and the day before. Then by a mathematical calculation (there are so many miles to a second or a minute) he finds the exact latitude. He sets his watch each day by the sun, and can thus tell, each day, the difference in time. The Chronometer is set and kept at Greenwich time, and comparing the watch, set by the sun each day with Greenwich time, he finds the longitude. Thus by latitude and longitude, he can find his exact position on a chart."[1]

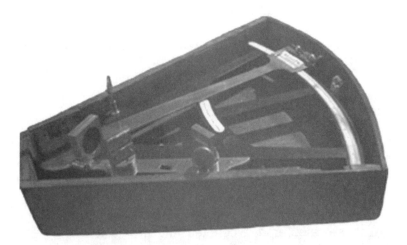

Sextant
Cape Cod National Seashore Salt Pond Visitor Center
Photo courtesy of Edward Weissberger

It was not always calm on the seas and a captain had to know the waters well and how to handle the sails to maintain course. There are frightening tales of storms and of cargo catching fire as ships and sailors made long, perilous journeys. On one such journey, Captain Bangs Hallet's cargo of cotton caught fire when the mast of his ship was struck by lightning during a storm.

Clipper ships were built for speed and they were the state of the art in ocean transport through the greater part of the 19th century. Indeed, the Clipper ship is said not to be a design but rather a state of mind. Many were constructed in Yarmouth and Dennis as well as elsewhere on Cape Cod. Large clipper ships sailed the Atlantic and to California via Cape Horn, a place of violent storms, high winds and treacherous waters. Rounding Cape Horn at the southern tip of South America was a dangerous journey, but the alternative totally overland route across North America to California and its gold or the combination sea and land route via Panama were equally perilous and far more arduous. It is worth noting that the iron, rolling stock and locomotives needed to build the Central Pacific portion of the transcontinental railroad after the Civil War came from the east coast on ships rounding Cape Horn.

In the 1840s, the American economy was booming. Foreign trade increased as demand for oriental goods including tea, silk and porcelain increased. With improved trade came inflation as shipping rates increased from ten dollars to sixty dollars a ton, an increase of 500 percent. At these rates, speed counted and it paid to design and build ships that delivered large cargoes in minimum time.

Clipper ships with Yankee sailors delivered the goods. Speeds from sixteen to eighteen knots, nautical miles per hour, were common and speeds up to twenty knots (23 miles per hour) were recorded.[b]

American clipper ships of the 1850s ranged in length from roughly 150 to 250 feet and carried a crew of twenty five to fifty sailors. The need for speed and the dangers of the sea made imposition of strict rules mandatory. While on the *National Eagle* with her sister, Mary Matthews Bray wrote:

---

[b] A nautical mile is 15 percent longer than the statute mile we generally use on land in the United States. A nautical mile is based on the earth's circumference and is the distance of one minute of arc measured on a great circle.

"A ship, far out to sea, is a little world in itself. All the work on board is carefully systematized. Each one has a part and is responsible for that part. The higher the rank, the greater the responsibility. One essential duty of a Captain is to make his passages from port to port, as short as possible with a due regard for safety. ... A 'lookout' must be kept to avoid collisions, and sails must be changed with changing winds, or reefed in sudden squalls. One of the mates, therefore, with a part of the crew, must be always on deck and on duty. ... There is always a man at the wheel, which is in the extreme aft part of the ship. His duty is to watch the compass in the binnacle before him, and to move his wheel accordingly. From his vantage ground there, however, he has an opportunity to see all that goes on in the vicinity. Forward of the main mast M and I are not allowed to go, but seclusion there would be impossible, for there the crew live and do most of their work."[2]

These beautiful, sleek ships were built to withstand the environment in which they sailed and some served for as many as forty-eight years. They were strongly built, with iron strapped over their frames and on the sides of the keel. But they required frequent maintenance and the damage suffered during an arduous crossing often meant costly repairs to spars, rigging, sails and fittings.

It was no small task sailing one of these great ships. The captain had to be constantly aware of what was happening on board, the changing weather and navigation. While the captain could determine his location in clear weather, navigation when clouds obscured the sun and stars required great skill, experience and knowledge of how the ship was performing. Many sails had to be attended to, changed, lowered or raised to keep the ship on course and out of danger as winds shifted and gained or diminished in strength. George Matthews, captain of the *National Eagle* on route to India, recorded in his log:

"Sunday, December 18. Commences with strong gales from east to E. S. E and cloudy weather. At four P. M. shortened sail to close reefs. At 8:30 P. M. furled jib, main sail, cross jack and spanker. The gale increasing, took in and furled the upper top-sails. Middle part, heavy gales, attended with squalls of wind and rain. At 1 A. M., carried away the main topmast stay-sail-stay. Had to run the ship before the wind, about an hour, to save the sail. At 3 A. M. Took in the fore-sail, and bore ship. At 4 A. M. the wind, shifted to the westward, and soon after fell calm. At 10 A. M. took a breeze again from about W. by S. Made all prudent sail. Ends brisk and clear from about West."[3]

Clipper Ship *Belle of the West*
Shiverick Shipyards, East Dennis
Thomas F. Hall, Captain
Photo from the Jim Carr collection

Captains

A young boy of age nine could find work on a ship and become a captain by age nineteen as often occurred in families where sailing was a way of life. Captain John Eldridge went to sea at age twelve and by the time he was a young man he captained his own packet ship. He was known for his strong, authoritarian voice which his crew, known as *Packet Rats*, dared not question.

Captain Frederick Howes, born in 1812, was the son of a sea captain. He began his working life as a cabinet maker but became a ship's captain at an early age. His greatest contribution was the invention of the *Howes Rig* which aided reefing of topsails and made it possible to sail a large ship with a smaller crew.

Captain Josiah Gorham, born in 1809, was one of five brothers; each became a ship's captain. He went to sea at fourteen and rose rapidly, commanding many ships out of Boston including the clipper ship *Kit Carson*. He was particularly well regarded for his business ability, another important skill needed by successful merchant mariners of the time. His acumen and taste are reflected in his home on Main Street in Yarmouth Port.

Captain Winthrop Sears, born in West Yarmouth in 1818, went to sea at the age of thirteen and was captain at age twenty-one. He commanded the ship *Conquest* and became captain of the steamer *Benjamin Franklin*, the pioneer ship of the Boston and Philadelphia line. When he retired from the sea at age fifty-five, he was elected to Yarmouth's board of selectmen and was director of the First National Bank of Yarmouth. A measure of the distinction and wealth men of the sea achieved can still be seen in the mansions they built throughout the Cape.

Shipwrights

The town of Dennis was an important center for construction of clipper ships. Asa Shiverick started his shipyard in 1820 at the location of today's Northside Marina and Dennis harbor on Sesuit Neck. With his sons, he built some of the finest ships ever launched on Cape Cod. The *Belle of the West*, 923 tons burthen[c], was built with a workforce of 21 men and launched by the Shivericks on March 25, 1853. They launched their last clipper ship, the *Ellen Sears*, 950 tons burthen, on June 2, 1863.

Also on the north side, the Brays owned a shipyard in the Hockanom section of Yarmouth where they built fishing schooners and sloops of up to 150 tons burthen, launching them into the Chase Garden River. From there, the as yet unrigged ships entered Cape Cod bay from the area now known as Bass Hole. Squire Elisha Doane also owned a large shipyard on the north side of Yarmouth, although it is not clear where it was located, and hired Isaiah Bray to work for him.

On the south side of Cape Cod, the Kelley family of South Yarmouth owned shipyards on the Bass River just north of where Route 28 crosses to Dennis. The Bass River was a busy shipping area with ships sailing to the West Indies, Boston, and the Southern States.

---

[c] Burthen is an antiquated measure used for most ships until approximately 1870 to describe the carrying capacity of a ship. As a capacity measure, it is not a measure of displacement and hence not a measure of buoyancy. Originally, it was an estimate of the amount of wine that could be carried. *To determine the burthen, ... of a ship, ... multiply the length of the keel into [by] the extreme breadth of the ship within-board, taken along the midship-beam, and multiply the product by the depth in the hold from the plank joining to the kelson upwards, to the main-deck, and divide the last product by 94, ...*
(See http://www.jcu.edu.au/aff/history/southseas/refs/falc/0239.html)

Packet Ships

The phrase packet ship doesn't really describe a ship at all. Rather, it connotes a type of service that began gaining popularity in the late 1700s. Before then, ships sailed when they had sufficient freight and or passengers on board. Packet ships pioneered the idea of sailing to a pre-announced schedule resulting in dramatically improved convenience for passengers and shippers alike. (See Appendix A for an example of a New York and Liverpool Packet schedule.)

Packet ships served communities up and down the east coast. Most of them were small ships designed to carry cargoes of the inter-coastal trade, such as salt, and to navigate in shallow and narrow channels. They were called *greyhounds of the sea*, as they were designed for speed in order to maintain schedules. People traveling to Boston and New York frequently went by packet ship as travel by sea was much more comfortable than overland routes on rough and often muddy roads aboard a *bone rattling* stagecoach.

Because they were used for both passengers and freight, packet ships were a good investment. Cape Cod merchants built their ships and then operated them on regular schedules between designated ports for a fixed fee, whether permitting. Prior to this, ships departed only after sufficient cargo and or passengers were on hand to make the journey profitable. Good business sense made for good profit. In 1818, the first scheduled packet ship sailed across the Atlantic, opening the door for packet lines such as the Black Ball Line which was the first to offer scheduled service across the Atlantic between New York and Liverpool. The Black Ball Line carried the majority of immigrants to the USA in the 19th century.[4]

More than one heaving or halyard chantey[d] memorializes this company and service on its ships.

Black Ball Line[5]

I served my time on the Black Ball line
To me way-ay-ay O Ri-o
On the Black Ball line I wasted me prime
Hurrah for the Black Ball line!

When a trim Black Ball liner's preparing for sea
To me way-ay-ay O Ri-o
You'll split your sides laughing such sights you would see
Hurrah for the Black Ball line!

There's tinkers and tailors, shoemakers and all
To me way-ay-ay O Ri-o
They're all shipped for sailors aboard the Black Ball
Hurrah for the Black Ball line!

When a big Black Ball liner's a-leaving her dock
To me way-ay-ay O Ri-o
The boys and the girls on the pier-head do flock
Hurrah for the Black Ball line!

Now, when the big liner, she's clear of land
To me way-ay-ay O Ri-o
Our bosun he roars out the word of command
Hurrah for the Black Ball line!

Come quickly, lay aft to the break of the poop
To me way-ay-ay O Ri-o
Or I'll help you along with the toe of me boot
Hurrah for the Black Ball line!

---

[d] Sea chanteys were rhythmic songs sailors used to help them work together on a common task.

Pay attention to orders, now, you one and all
To me way-ay-ay O Ri-o
For see high above there flies the Black Ball
Hurrah for the Black Ball line!

'Tis larboard and starboard, on deck you will sprawl
To me way-ay-ay O Ri-o
For kicking Jack Rogers commands the Black Ball
Hurrah for the Black Ball line!

Within ten years, ships were being designed for greater speed in order to meet pre-announced schedules. By 1850, packets were America's best way to travel.

The packets were indeed a Cape Cod product. The timber to build them came from nearby forests and they were sailed by Cape Cod captains and crews. Often a town had more than one packet, making two or three round trip voyages to Boston each week. These ships were the pride of their owners and were kept in fine working order. Attention was paid to beauty and comfort as well as performance. The schooner *Postboy*, of Truro, had a cabin made of solid mahogany and bird's-eye maple. The draperies were of fine silk. Often a spirit of competition developed among ship owners and captains of various towns. Each tried to outdo the other in speed, size or beauty of their ships.

Travel aboard packet ships must have been interesting, to say the least. On average, twenty-five to fifty passengers were on board and a trip to Boston took anywhere from six to 48 hours, depending on difficulties along the way. Meals were eaten on board for a fee of twenty-five cents and the round trip cost $1.50. In Yarmouth, news of a packet's return was signaled by a flag flying on the highest hill.

Extended travel on board ship was a true adventure. Ellen M. Knights, while on the brig[e] *Colorado* sailing from Boston to Valparaiso around Cape Horn between 1849 and 1850, described daily life. In her interesting letter to Mr. Ira Edwin, she also wrote of frightening weather, vessels encountered and a wedding that took place during the trip. (See Appendix B for this letter.)

Town Dock, on Yarmouth's north side, was built in the 1790s at Bass Hole. However, as is the way with Cape Cod land, sand silted in the area making it too shallow for packet ships. To solve this serious commercial problem, Yarmouth formed Yarmouth Port. At that time Yarmouth Port extended from where the fire station on Route 6A is now located, west to Barnstable. Not until the 1960s did Yarmouth's Bass Hole area become part of Yarmouth Port when the two post offices were merged into one.

In 1832, Central Wharf was built at the end of Central Street, which is now known as Wharf Lane. Remains of the wharf are still visible. Central Wharf was a very busy place. Horse drawn buggies waited with passengers ready to board ship. People waited for shipments and visitors wandered about. Children ran down the streets and alleys. Shipwrights collected lumber while other businessmen retrieved their newly arrived merchandise. Consumers purchased products at the general store located on the wharf. It was an exciting and profitable time.

---

[e] The Random House Dictionary of the English Language defines a brig as *a two-masted vessel square-rigged on both masts.*

Ropewalks and Rigging

Rope was an essential product for shipping and the cordage industry was a prosperous one on Cape Cod during the maritime days. The Bass River area had a ropewalk built by David Kelley and Sylvanus Crowell in 1802. On the north side, Squire Doane, always ready to make a profit, built a ropewalk close to his tavern, near where today's playground is located in the triangle formed by the intersection of Old Kings Highway (also known as Main Street and Route 6A,) Playground Lane, and Old Church Street.

Ropewalks were long buildings of up to nine hundred feet that contained a spinning shed. A horse turned a heavy wheel to spin the rope. A person spinning hemp attached one end of the hemp to the spinning wheel and wrapped the bundle of hemp around his waist. While walking backwards down the long building, the spinner fed the hemp through his fingers as the turning wheel twisted the rope. Ropewalks often had tarring sections as some of the more inexpensive rope had to be tarred in order to protect it from water and weather. Tarring of rope was a risky business as tarring sheds often burned, destroying the associated ropewalk. Cordage was sold by weight.

Mostly men and boys worked in ropewalks where salary was determined by one's experience. Salary might mean cash, or cash and food, or cash and lodging, or cash and rum. Squire Doane was known for paying with rum. Squire Elisha Doane's business integration was unusual in that he not only owned the ropewalk, but he also owned the tavern and was president of the Yarmouth Temperance Society. One can only wonder at the conflicts of interest he faced.

Work in ropewalks was long and hard. A standard ten hour workday paid about eighty cents on average, but in those days seventy-five cents bought a full dinner. Ropewalks were not heated and were shut down when the weather turned particularly cold.

Cordage making on Cape Cod was a prosperous business until two things happened. First, competition was introduced by the Plymouth Cordage Company in 1824 and second, railroads changed the way goods and materials were transported, disrupting the shipping industry which in turn reduced the need for cordage. The Plymouth Cordage Company used machines and new technology to produce cordage faster and cheaper than that produced in the small, labor intensive businesses on Cape Cod. Waterpower, more readily available in Plymouth than on the Cape, facilitated use of machinery. Faster, cheaper manufacturing allowed the Plymouth Cordage Company to establish dominance in the business and drive out less efficient Cape Cod businesses. Plymouth Cordage Company's business practice of paying retired shipmasters commissions for referred business also contributed to the demise of the Cape's cordage industry.

The Plymouth Cordage Company remained active for one hundred and twenty five years through depressions and two world wars with steady and strong business management. The spinning of rope in Yarmouth came to an end in 1848 when the primary customers, the packet ships, were supplanted by the railroads.

End Of An Era

Clipper ships on the high seas faded from existence with the introduction of steamships. Steamships were able to carry more goods at reduced cost on more reliable schedules resulting in reduced freight rates. Trade quickly moved from wind power to steam power, ultimately resulting in the demise of both clipper ships and packet ships. Shipwrights closed their shipyards. The Shiverick shipyard in Dennis became a guano[f] storage plant. On April 22, 1871, the *Yarmouth Register* reported:

> "The Schooner H.S. Barnes will sail for Boston via Provincetown on Monday next, taking two fishing crews to the latter place. She is to be sold in Boston, and this ought, if it does not, end the packets service between this port and Boston. ... There are to be found plenty of citizens who cling conservatively to the old ways and are always ready to argue money out of the pockets of old capitalists to sustain the packet enterprise ... but patronage is out of the question and the last few years have proved money invested in this manner to be spent in vain."

The rapidity with which steam replaced wind as a means to power ships was a consequence of many factors. Larger vessels facilitated by steam power were more cost effective than sailing vessels. Because steamships supplied their own power, rather than relying on the weather, they could go where they wanted, when they wanted, a great advantage to those attempting to maintain a schedule. While transatlantic steam shipping began in Britain, steam powered shipping was soon a factor in

---

[f] The Random House Dictionary of the English Language defines guano as
   1. a natural manure composed chiefly of the excrement of sea birds,
   2. any similar substance, as an artificial fertilizer made from fish

United States waters. As early as 1838, two British steamships crossed the Atlantic.

Steamships

Edward Knight Collins, born on Cape Cod in Truro, began his shipping career when only fifteen years old. Following similar actions of Cunard in Britain, he obtained funding from the United States Congress in support of the United States Mail Steamship Company by convincing Congress that steamships were necessary to carry mail and, in time of war, troops. Collins followed in the footsteps of captains such as Asa Eldridge when his steamship *Atlantic* set a crossing record on her maiden voyage. In 1854, with Britain engaged in the Crimean war and Cunard obliged to transport troops, Collins' company gained supremacy on the Atlantic run. Alas, tragedy struck when two of Collins' ships were lost at sea. Once Cunard was free from war responsibilities and Collins was unable to obtain renewed Congressional funding, the United States Mail Steamship Company went out of business.

Soon, steamships pervaded all of shipping. John Ericsson, a Swedish inventor who worked in both Britain and the United States, recognized the advantage of screw propulsion in comparison to paddlewheel propulsion on the open seas and designed the first propeller driven commercial ship. His propulsion system was accepted for commercial steamers and in 1844 by the United States Navy which built the *USS Princeton* as the first screw propelled war vessel. In the early days of the American Civil War, Ericsson designed and built the ironclad *USS Monitor* in a remarkably short 118 days. Following the historic battle between the North's *Monitor* and the South's

ironclad *CSS Virginia*, formerly the *USS Merrimack*, at Hampton Roads in March, 1862, Ericsson continued to design and build iron clad steamships.

One of the most remarkable of iron clad ships was the *CSS Albemarle*, constructed in 1864. Designed by John L. Porter and built by Gilbert Elliott at Edward's Ferry on the Roanoke River, the *Albemarle* was 122 feet long, and had a draft of eight feet. The planking was four inches thick over 8x10 inch frames. The central shield was sixty feet long covered by two layers of two inch iron plating.

Though ship building and shipping were no longer mainstays of its economy, Cape Cod continued to play a role on the sea beyond coastal fishing. In December, 1930, the world's first diesel powered ship designed specifically for oceanographic research was delivered by its Danish builders to the Woods Hole Oceanographic Institution (WHOI). The 350 ton *Atlantis* played a key role in that institution's rise to pre-eminence in the study of the sea.

The mini-submarine *Alvin*, built for the Woods Hole Oceanographic Institution in the early 1960s, was instrumental in the discovery of the wreck of the *Titanic*, and today WHOI continues its active research and discovery roles throughout the world's oceans.

Woods Hole Oceanographic Institution
Docked Research Vessels
Photo by Doug Weisman; Photo courtesy of *The Register*

From Water to Rails

Though packet ships were the preferred mode of travel along the east coast in the early part of the 1800s, bumpy, dusty stagecoaches also made regular runs to and from Cape Cod. Inn-keepers relied on stagecoaches to bring them weary travelers in need of rest and refreshment and made a handsome profit from these services. On January 25, 1838, the *Yarmouth Register* wrote:

A stage will leave Sears Arms Hotel, Yarmouth Port, for Boston every day, Sundays excepted, at 11:00 o'clock A.M. and arrive from Boston every day, Sundays excepted, at 6 and a half o'clock P.M. All baggage at the risk of the owner.

Stagecoach Typical of the Times
This stagecoach ran between Cicero and Syracuse, NY
Photo courtesy of the author

The Sears Arms Hotel was located at the corner of today's Summer Street and Main Street and is now the Cape Cod Inn. The Old Yarmouth Inn, built in 1696 and located on Main Street next to where the Cape Cod Inn now stands, was the base of stagecoach operations in the 1700s. From there, coaches departed for Chatham and Provincetown as well as Boston.

Introduction of railroads to Cape Cod came early and rapidly. A line that reached Sandwich in 1848 was extended to Yarmouth Port and Hyannis in 1854, Orleans in 1861, and Provincetown in 1872. Not only did the railroads offer a faster, more reliable and more comfortable mode of transportation for people, they offered faster transportation for increased quantities of commerce. Railroads contributed to the doom of packet ships and inter-city stagecoach travel as well.

Many sectors of the American economy boomed because of railroads along with the railroad industry itself. According to Robert H. Farson in his book *Cape Cod Railroads:*

> "... from the 1870s until 1900, railroads provided inexpensive transportation that in one generation made possible the settling of America, a huge land area that Thomas Jefferson said would take a thousand years."[6]

Railroad travel made Cape Cod accessible to tourists, opening the Cape to a new industry that today remains critical to the livelihood of many of the Cape's residents. Via the Cape Cod Railroad and its connection to other lines, travelers could reach the Cape from anywhere in the country within a few short days.

In 1854, the Cape Cod Branch Railroad offered three round trips a day between Boston and Hyannis and in that year carried 95,000 passengers. Toward the end of 1854, a railroad wharf was completed in Hyannis, an asset for those traveling between Hyannis and Nantucket, allowing them to switch from steamship to train without intermediate travel. The wharf quickly became the central area for shipping as it facilitated transport of trade goods between sea and land. Economically, the wharf was an incredible boost to the railroad and because of a booming trade industry, it processed imports valued at $557,700 in 1893.[9]

---

[9] Long term inflation rates allowing comparison of currency value in any given year to that of 2002 are difficult to estimate prior to the introduction of the Consumer Price Index in 1913. However, inflation factors as far back as 1665 have been estimated.
(See http://oregonstate.edu/Dept/pol_sci/fac/sahr/sahr.htm)
Based on inflation factors available from this publication, $557,700 in 1893 is the equivalent of $11,154,000 in 2002.

At the end of the Civil War in 1865, the Cape Cod Railroad generated a total income of $124,891 in passenger travel, a large sum at the time. Of great significance, railroads made seasonal travel to Cape Cod from Boston and other areas possible. In 1867, a new locomotive named *Highland Light* was inaugurated and advertised as the finest built. Painted red and blue and pulling a stream of yellow and green cars, it must have been an impressive sight as it wound along Cape Cod's tracks.

Cape Cod's Early Trains
Built in 1848 by Hinkley and Drury of Boston
This engine weighed 25 tons
Photo from the collection of Howard D. Goodwin; Photo courtesy of *The Register*

It wasn't long before widespread commuting came into existence. Short commutes by horse had long been possible but very impractical. Inclement weather, the need to care for one's horse, bad roads and slow speed all mitigated against regular commuting between home and work. Prior to the railroad, one only infrequently worked any significant distance from one's home. Railroads changed that, making it possible to commute significant distances between home and office in comfort. Special commuter tariffs were established allowing people to travel back and forth using season tickets at rates reduced from single trip rates. Season tickets also helped turn Cape Cod into a vacation resort. More and more people came to enjoy the Cape's assets.

As early as 1871, tourism, a new industry predicated on leisure time, discretionary funds and rapid transportation, was becoming a significant contributor to Cape Cod's economy with railroads supplying the transportation. Summertime weekend train service between New York's Grand Central Station and Cape Cod began in 1925. Weekend trips by train took on a party atmosphere. Acquaintances were made, music was played and everyone enjoyed their weekend excursion. This service lasted for thirty-nine years, ending in 1964, and it was another twenty-two years before Amtrak reinstated the service with its first train pulling into Hyannis in June, 1986.

At the same time that railroads were bringing tourists to Cape Cod, automobiles and modern roads came into existence, bringing yet another mode of comfortable, rapid transportation along with a huge associated industry. Automobiles allowed people to come and go as they pleased, not in any way dependent on someone else's schedule or routing.

From Railways to Roadways

In an article published in 1959, *The Register* reported:

> "The Railway Express office closed in July as freight trains stopped rumbling into Depot Square, replaced by truck trailers. Train service from Boston was discontinued July 1."

Once again technology changed life and travel on Cape Cod as a faster pace of daily living took hold. The new way to travel while on Cape Cod was to drive the Mid-Cape Highway. *The Register* article continues that the town ... *was getting carloads of people coming down from Boston just to spend a few hours.*

This portion of the old railroad tracks is now the bike tunnel in Eastham.

Photo courtesy of the Cape Cod National Seashore

Eastham Railroad in 1959
This portion of the railroad is now part of the bike railtrail
Photo courtesy of *The Register*

State roads on the Cape were constructed in bits and pieces. In 1895, stretches of roadway were put down on both the north and south sides of Yarmouth. Travel on these early, unpaved roads was quite different from what we enjoy today because roads were dusty and full of ruts, making travel dirty, bumpy and difficult. Later, when macadam roads replaced dirt roads, travel became far more enjoyable. Automobiles suffered less wear and tear and it became unnecessary to spray water on the roads in an effort to reduce dust. Still, macadam roads did need to be oiled.[h] In the early 1900s, as the first motor cars began to appear, cross-cape roads were built connecting the north and south sides.

In 1905, three types of automobile, gasoline, steam and electric, shared the roads with horse-drawn carriages. Clearly, rules were needed to prevent accidents. A car suddenly passing a horse could frighten the horse, causing an unpleasant experience for horse and rider alike.

Most villages had water pumps that were used by residents to gather water for home use or to quench their thirst on a hot, sunny afternoon. The pumps were also used for watering horses and with the introduction of steam powered automobiles, they were used to draw water for cars. Automobiles, even though convenient, soon caused significant problems and it wasn't long before selectmen felt it necessary to deal with speeding cars and intoxicated drivers. In 1911 the first police bylaws were drafted.

---

[h] The Random House Dictionary of the English Language defines macadamize as *paving by laying and compacting successive layers of broken stone. Oiling these roads helped preserve and stabilize them.*

Yarmouth Port Town Pump
Photo courtesy of Edward Weissberger

Continuing technological development altered life on the Cape. Introduction and macadamizing of roads were main contributors to increased property values which rose by one million dollars from 1890 to 1914. An increasing population made possible by improved transportation and mechanization required more modern conveniences.

Communication of news and business information became more important to both citizens and town businesses. Telegraph service began on Cape Cod in 1855 followed by the first telephone in 1883. Yarmouth's first telephone exchange was installed in Hallet's Drug Store on Old Kings Highway in Yarmouth Port in 1898. Amazingly, people could talk to friends and relatives and could communicate with businessmen in Europe in less time than it took to communicate with people in Sandwich just a few years earlier. By 1907, telephone conversations had become an essential component of daily life. Doctors installed telephones and since people wanted to reach their doctor quickly when they became ill, phones became common household appliances.

Cape Cod's resident and tourist populations were both increasing. With road improvements, more visitors traveled to the Cape and awakened to the beauty and peacefulness of the shore. Cape Cod became the prestigious resort area. A 1900 article in *The Register* suggested that the recovery from lost population of earlier years was due to summer resort businesses. The article went on to state that this could lead to permanent residence for some people. Eventually, people began to lengthen their stay and the visiting season extended to include spring and fall, often called shoulder seasons.

Most summer visitors congregated near the water and permanent residents adjacent to the more popular areas began to have misgivings about what summer vacationers meant for them. A letter published in *The Register* in January, 1906, described concerns pertinent to South Yarmouth:

> "The question is, shall we keep the Town Landing given to us by our predecessors or shall we make concessions to please those who have recently come among us and bought real estate bordering the river, putting dwellings thereon that they may abide with us during the summer season? While they are welcome to mingle with us and

we would make their sojourn as pleasant as possible, yet they should not expect that we will sacrifice those rights that have been held so long as a great privilege to the people, and far more now because about all the land bordering on the river is owned by summer visitors, making it almost impossible to get to the water-front without trespassing, except by the way that we yet hold, leading to the town landings."[7]

Encouraging tourists has always been a double edged sword for Cape Codders.

In spite of tourist related issues, Cape Codders wanted economic growth and development to continue. Summer visitors provided jobs and many yearly residents appreciated the newcomers' desire to spend time on Cape Cod. Brochures were printed to attract visitors to Yarmouth and the mid-Cape area. It wasn't long before business minded people began thinking about providing accommodations for summer residents. The Englewood Beach Hotel opened in West Yarmouth in 1901. The next year brought the building of Aberdeen Hall, also in West Yarmouth. This hotel had all the finest features available, including telephones. As building continued, West Yarmouth became a real estate developer's delight. Business was definitely picking up on Cape Cod. Even though reports of economic depression appeared in local newspapers, service and support industries expanded. In particular, energy distribution for natural gas and electricity became common. New hotels were planned and boating facilities built along the Bass River.

The stock market crash of 1929 was followed by a serious national downturn and *The Great Depression*. In June 1931, deterioration of the Cape's economy became apparent with the closing of the American Metallic Fabric Company, a producer of wire mesh belting for the paper industry. By 1934, unemployment had become a serious issue on Cape Cod and citizens appreciated help, whatever its source. On February 13, a Yarmouth Town Meeting resolution of commendation was voted and sent to President Franklin Roosevelt saying:

> Resolved, that we, the citizens of the Town of Yarmouth, Massachusetts, in annual town meeting assembled, do extend to you our grateful appreciation for the effort made through the creation of the Civil Works Administration bringing employment to many of our worthy citizens when no other work was to be had.[8]

The Works Progress Administration (WPA) was very helpful to many who were able to find work improving schools and parks and even working on the Cape Cod Canal project. In 1936, things began to improve. Tourism increased and businesses again turned a profit. This was good news for the American Metallic Fabric Company. In 1937 it was in operation once again.

The Cape Cod Canal Project

Constructing a canal across Cape Cod was not a simple matter. Such a canal had been discussed, planned and abandoned many times before it was finally brought to fruition. As early as 1632, Miles Standish of Plymouth Colony considered a canal. Even George Washington recognized that a canal connecting Cape Cod Bay and Buzzards Bay would be advantageous for security reasons. Skill, insight and business sense were all needed to make this project succeed and the men who brought the Cape Cod Canal into existence had these qualities along with inventiveness and creativity.

August Perry Belmont, born in 1853, was an exceptionally innovative, creative individual from a remarkable family. It was he who first thought of placing spikes on running shoes to improve traction. The idea stuck and this type of shoe is now standard at track events.

Belmont's mother was from the Perry family of Bourne. His maternal grandfather was Commodore Matthew Calbraith Perry who was critically influential in opening trade between Japan and the United States. Captain Oliver Hazard Perry, also of Belmont's family, was a hero in the Battle of Lake Erie in 1813 during the War of 1812. Belmont's father was a very successful businessman who worked with J. P. Morgan and owned a banking house known as August Belmont and Company. August Perry Belmont became president of this company when his father died in 1890. Because the company worked with railroad bonds, Belmont became interested in transportation. This interest led to his becoming director of the Wright Company which manufactured airplanes in association with Wilbur and Orville who flew the first airplane at Kitty Hawk, North Carolina, on December 17, 1903.

Belmont's interest in sports also led him in prestigious and prosperous directions. Farson wrote:

> "... he bred thoroughbreds, the most notable of which was Man O' War, built Belmont Park, founded the American Kennel Club, and twice helped build yachts that defended America's Cup against British challengers ... He was director of both the Metropolitan Opera and the Metropolitan Museum of Art."[9]

As time went on, Belmont became involved in planning and building the first subway line in New York City which began operation in 1904. While working on this project, he met William Barclay Parsons, the engineer in charge of the subway project. Parsons was made of the same cloth as Belmont and was usually involved in more than one project. In 1904, he headed to Panama as one of the commission members planning construction of the Panama Canal. Parsons' proposal for a canal without locks was out-voted and so he returned to the United States in 1905. He, Belmont and a man named Michael J. Degnon soon came together to work on the often considered canal project for Cape Cod. August Perry Belmont envisioned the canal as not only a profitable venture, but also as a memorial to his mother's heritage.

Reasons for building the Cape Cod Canal were three-fold. First was to decrease the risk of ships being wrecked on the dangerous shores of the Cape, second was to shorten the distance between Cape Cod Bay and southern waters thereby saving shipping time and third was to enhance profits for the shipping industry. The canal's merits included bringing more business to the shipping industry and improving national defense by making it easier, faster and safer for coastal vessels to travel north and south during emergencies.

Belmont and his colleagues began by considering problems they would face in building the canal. Again, Parsons pushed for a sea-level, no-lock canal believing that tidal flow would scrub the canal, thereby minimizing maintenance efforts and costs. They recognized that boulders in the shallows of Cape Cod shores would make dredging difficult and costly. Nevertheless, they concluded that although construction would be complicated and expensive, there would be sufficient shipping through the canal to return a profit. Further, they concluded that the canal would have minimal impact on railroad profits as railroads were busy enough and did not care to transport low paying bulk freight so easily carried by ship.

Belmont obtained funding for the canal by forming two companies, the Cape Cod Construction Company and the Boston, Cape Cod and New York Canal Company. A system of stock and bond securities traded within the syndicate Belmont organized around these companies, in combination with bonds sold to Belmont's friends, generated sufficient capital to build the canal. No securities were sold to the public.

On May 15, 1909, contracts were signed to begin excavating the canal. On June 19, ships arrived laden with granite, the first installment of what would eventually become a three-thousand foot long breakwater. Rising eight feet above high tide, this breakwater was designed to protect the canal's east entrance from fierce Atlantic storms.

Belmont was determined to make this project work, but people of Cape Cod were not yet ready to trust it. Canal projects had been abandoned too many times before for them to believe that this endeavor would be successful. On August 2, dredging began on the approach channels. One dredge, the *Kennedy,* removed one million cubic yards of material in only twenty-six months without working in winter. That material was put on scows and dumped at sea. The *Kennedy*, an old ladder type dredge, worked twenty-four hours a day and had a crew of twenty six men.

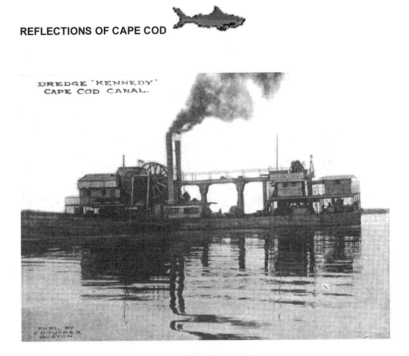

Dredge *Kennedy*
Photo courtesy of *The Register*

Typical of Cape Cod weather, sudden gales brought disasters and caused canal progress to fall behind schedule. In addition, digging equipment sank in swamps and being ungainly, had difficulty moving on rough ground. Even with all this difficulty, construction moved forward and by September, 1910, considerable progress had been made.

Three bridges for railroad and automobile traffic were required, and the Canal Company signed a contract to ensure their timely construction. The railroad bridge and the Bourne Bridge span the canal toward the western end with the Sagamore Bridge toward the east. The railroad bridge was finished and in use by November, 1911. Construction of the first Bourne Bridge, just east of the railroad bridge, began in August, 1910. This bridge, ready for use in May, 1911, did not look then as it does today as it was an electrically operated drawbridge with a single track for trolleys. Approach roads to the bridge were completed in October of that same year. The Sagamore bridge was ready for use in 1913. All three bridges had a nominal channel width of 160 feet and main bridge piers were sunk deep enough to allow for future expansion. Finally, with considerable excitement, service on the canal began July 29, 1914.

Old Bourne Bridge
Notice the Wooden Fenders protecting the Piers
The current Bourne Bridge is superimposed in the background
Photo courtesy of Donald Jacobs

Navigating the canal was not without difficulty. Wooden protection fenders in front and to the sides of the piers were installed to prevent bridge damage in the event of ships colliding with the piers. This decreased the channel passage by twenty feet to only 140 feet, too narrow to permit easy two-way traffic. Rapid tidal flow combined with the narrow passage led to numerous accidents.

Cape Codders and visitors alike found the canal's daily activities interesting. Watching this activity became a popular social event. Two sister ships, the *Boston* and the *New York*, ran daily service between Boston and New York with the *New York* being the main attraction. People gathered to see the ship pass through the canal. Not only was it exciting to see the ship that had left Boston in the evening arrive at the Sandwich entrance only three hours later, it was an enjoyable gathering of friends and neighbors.

Although construction of the Cape Cod Canal was a success, the canal was a financial disaster for Belmont. Expectations had been that coastal tow ships would generate a profit to the canal company. Unfortunately, this profit failed to materialize. Even though the canal facilitated increased box barge traffic between Cape Cod Bay and Buzzards Bay, only twenty percent of possible shipping business made use of the canal. Tolls were raised in 1923 but income still continued to decline in 1924. Use of the canal continued to drop in 1925. Expenses were rising and surplus funds shrinking.

Federal government control of the canal first occurred during World War I. After the *Perth Amboy* was sunk by a German submarine off Orleans, President Wilson ordered Belmont to allow government operation of the canal. However, full control of the canal did not occur until 1927. The proposed federal Rivers and Harbors Act of 1917, which included an amendment that the Cape Cod Canal be purchased by the United States Government in order to ensure the canal's financial viability, was tabled.

When Calvin Coolidge became president in 1923, he pushed Congress to pass the canal bill. Although the bill failed in the House of Representatives, Coolidge pressed on. Finally, in June of 1926, the House passed a rivers and harbors act that included purchasing the canal and the bill passed the Senate in January, 1927. People working for the Canal Company now had a new boss, the United States Government.

Even though the canal was a losing financial battle, August Perry Belmont's interest in the Cape Cod Canal never ceased. When he died on December 10, 1924, following surgery for blood poisoning, the canal had been in operation for ten years. Farson wrote:

> "Belmont's lifetime record of success, particularly in transportation, had fallen with the Cape Cod Canal. He approached the canal with the Midas touch; it turned to lead. Belmont had put more money into the canal than anyone, and he lost about $1 million in cash on his original investment. His actual loss was about $5 million, the amount he could have earned by investing his $1 million elsewhere. When he died, after spending eighteen years of his life on the project, Belmont left behind a crumbling dream, a waterway even the spendthrift government did not want."[10]

In spite of this, Belmont did leave his legacy and a monument to his mother's heritage, so in this way his dream had come true.

Eventually it became necessary to redesign and rebuild the canal in order to accommodate significant shipping and reduce accidents. When the government took over in 1927, the Army Corps of Engineers already knew that improvements were needed. By 1928 all tolls were eliminated making the waterway much more attractive to the shipping industry. Studies were undertaken and questionnaires mailed, all designed to gain an understanding of required improvements. One of the most needed improvements, and the most expensive one at that, was the need to facilitate two-way traffic and enhance safety. Accomplishing this required a wider, deeper channel with replacement of all three bridges. The new Bourne and Sagamore highway bridges had to be elevated enough for tall ships to pass beneath while still allowing vehicular traffic continually to cross them. The stationary railroad bridge was replaced by one that rides up and down on towers, thereby allowing ships to pass under and trains to cross on demand. Highway bridge work began in 1933; both highway bridges were completed and ready for use on June 21, 1935.

Sagamore Bridge with Two Way Canal Traffic
Photo courtesy of Edward Weissberger

The opening of the new Cape Cod Canal bridges was an exciting time with parades and celebrations. *The Register* reported that

> "James Michael Curley cut the ribbon at the Bourne Bridge and the widow of the canal's founder, August Belmont, did the honors at the Sagamore."

With humor, The Register continued that

> "... paraders numbered 8,000 and more than 100,000 were said to line the route. The steady stream crossing the canal has never let up."

New Railroad Bridge
Photo Courtesy of Edward Weissberger

Upon completion of the three new bridges, the eastern portion of Cape Cod became efficiently connected to the rest of the world by well paved roads making Cape Cod easily accessible by automobile. Once over the bridge, however, people had to drive on narrow, winding state roads. The first construction phase of today's Mid-Cape Highway opened in 1950 as a single, two lane macadam road running from the Sagamore bridge to Route 132 in Hyannis. This highway allowed travelers to go from the bridge to the Cape's center in half the time it took to travel the same distance on Old Kings Highway. In 1954, today's east-bound lane of the Mid-Cape Highway was completed and the Cape's first divided highway was ready for use. In 1955, two lanes were completed from Route 132 in Hyannis to Route 134 in Dennis. Connecting Boston and Cape Cod via the Mid-Cape Highway made day trips reasonably easy, a crucial factor for the expanding tourist economy.

---

[1] A Sea Trip In Clipper Ship Days, Mary Matthews Bray, page 68.

[2] A Sea Trip In Clipper Ship Days, Mary Matthews Bray, pages 73, 74 and 75.

[3] A Sea Trip in Clipper Ship Days, Mary Matthews Bray, page 28.

[4] http://www.tradingstories.com/blacballincl.html

[5] http://www.speakeasy.org/~anitra/chanteys/blackball.html

[6] Cape Cod Railroads, Robert H. Farson, Introduction.

[7] The Town of Yarmouth, Massachusetts: A History, 1639-1989, Marion Vuilleumier, page 71.

[8] The Town of Yarmouth, Massachusetts: A history, 1639-1989, Marion Vuilleumier, page 127.

[9] The Cape Cod Canal, Robert H. Farson, page 30.

[10] The Cape Cod Canal, Robert H. Farson, page 62, 63.

CHAPTER 3:
GROWING TOWNS, ECONOMIC CHALLENGES, LIFE AND DEATH

Cape Cod Towns

L et's go back to the beginning. In the year 1620, Plymouth was settled as a plantation by Pilgrims and Strangers after a perilous Atlantic crossing on the *Mayflower.* Pilgrim Separatists sought religious freedom from the Church of England while Strangers, although they did not adhere to the same religious beliefs as the Pilgrim Separatists, had skills needed by the community. Ten years later, in 1630, the Massachusetts Bay Colony to the north was settled by Puritans. While contention between the two settlements existed, Plymouth Plantation and Massachusetts Bay Colony generally cooperated with one another and when the Bay Colony needed additional land for farming and livestock, it was sold to the Bay Colony by Plymouth Plantation. People also moved from Massachusetts Bay to Plymouth Plantation in search of economic opportunity and religious tolerance. By 1635, the population of Plymouth Plantation had considerably grown. Still, with the influx of Puritans who arrived with the Winthrop Fleet in the 1630s, the Massachusetts Bay Colony grew far faster than the Plymouth Colony and, in 1692, absorbed the smaller colony.

By 1636, Plymouth Plantation had grown sufficiently with the addition of Duxbury and Scituate to become a colony rather than a plantation. Expansion to the southeast continued and by 1639 Plymouth had grown to include seven towns and settlements: Duxbury, Scituate, Plymouth, Sandwich, Barnstable, Yarmouth and Nauset which later became Eastham.

Sandwich, Barnstable and Yarmouth, three of the seven towns of Plymouth Colony, were established on Cape Cod with many of the residents having come from Massachusetts Bay Colony. Growth and diversification brought problems during the late 1630s as the Cape was still a part of Plymouth Colony and was bound to Plymouth's political and economic system. Sandwich was the first community settled and by 1638 it had a fairly large population. Next came Barnstable and Yarmouth. Migration to these towns was not only due to population growth but also was in response to religious conflict. Even though people moved to the Cape to avoid religious conflict, issues of religious practice frequently followed them.

In 1639, John Crow, Thomas Howes and Anthony Thacher established homes in Mattacheese. Only a year later, 28 families called this community home, a population sufficient to establish the community as a town, and the name was changed to Yarmouth. During these times a town could not be formed without a church and a minister. Yarmouth's first minister of the First Congregational Church was Marmaduke Matthews. The last town founded on the Cape as part of Plymouth Colony was Eastham, where Pilgrims had first encountered Native People in 1620. When formed as a town in 1646, it was named Nauset and remained Nauset until 1651 when the court, the legislature of the time, declared that it would be called Eastham.

Two major problems existed in Yarmouth's early days; land ownership and religious issues. One troublesome factor was that members of the Congregational Church had the right to state their opinions regarding the affairs of the church. This caused many conflicts within the congregation and presented uncomfortable situations for the minister.

Land ownership disputes were finally resolved when the court of Plymouth Colony assigned Myles Standish the task of supervising land distributions in Yarmouth. Standish did his work well and by 1648 most land issues had been resolved.

Colonial Yarmouth had different boundaries from the Yarmouth we know today. When settled in 1639, Yarmouth included today's village of Cummaquid to the west and bordered on Barnstable. The eastern boundary was not clearly defined until 1646 with the formation of Nauset, later Eastham. The region we now know as Dennis was part of Yarmouth and did not become an independent town until it gained sufficient population to establish a church in 1793.

Daily Life And Childhood

Daily life includes working, practicing beliefs and striving for ideals. Each of these activities stands alone and yet each is intermingled with the others to make us who we are. These activities, practiced by many people, give a town a life of its own. People tend to settle in areas where others share the same beliefs and life style. Likewise, the area where people settle shapes their lives and how they go about living their daily lives. For example, Cape Cod houses have evolved in response to the Cape's environment as well as people's changing needs. Even in colonial times, Cape Cod houses were built with steep roofs to protect against wind and when feasible faced south to enhance solar warming. Also, many occupations of people who chose to live on the Cape are closely associated with characteristics of the Cape.

1700s Yarmouth Port House
Photo courtesy of Edward Weissberger.

Beliefs, such as the Puritan way of life, impacted behavior and how parents raised their children. Beliefs, occupations and activities change with the times as do parental behavior and childhood activities. Routine family life in the 1600s, 1700s and 1800s was dramatically different from family life as we enjoy it today.

A child's home in Puritan times was often cold and drafty, especially in winter. Summer was generally pleasant with warm days and cool evenings but as is true for New

England in general, winter can be quite a different story. A mother bathed and dressed her infant in front of a warm hearth but when she turned away and carried her child to another room, the infant was exposed to cold, bone chilling air because there was no direct heating of rooms without a fireplace.

Baptism was one of a baby's first rituals. Meeting Houses were not heated in winter and could be uncomfortably cold. There are stories of winter baptisms when water in the christening basin was frozen and the ice had to be broken for the ceremony. Weather was not considered when it came to religious duties. Babies were baptized, dressed in linen and wrapped only in a christening blanket. Records of the times show that some babies *died of being baptized* referring to these extremely cold conditions.

During colonial times, when a child's mother participated in an activity at the meeting house, she frequently brought her child along as going to the meeting house was a large part of a woman's life. Families were large with as many as twelve to fifteen children born to one family, but many children did not live past infancy. Of those children who survived infancy, many did not reach adulthood. From a family of twelve or fifteen children, it was not uncommon for only three to outlive their parents.

Cradles in the 1700s were made with a hooded area at one end to protect the infant from drafts. If twins were born, a single cradle was used but a hooded area was present at each end with the twins lying in opposite directions. Superstitions of the time concerning how to protect and raise babies were followed, including such protocols as putting silver and gold in a child's hands so that wealth and social standing would come to him or her in adulthood.

Baby Cradle
Cape Cod National Seashore Salt Pond Visitor Center
Photo courtesy of Edward Weissberger

Viewed in the light of today's medical knowledge and techniques, colonial medical remedies are often seen as having done more harm than good. Some of the illnesses that could beset an infant were worms, and, of course, teething pain. Ingestion of snails and sometimes earthworms was prescribed. Alice Morse Earle writes of one remedy for rickets, a childhood disease resulting in skeletal deformities now understood to be due to lack of dietary vitamin D and calcium:

> "The admirable and most famous Snail water. Take a peck of garden Shel Snails, wash them well in Small Beer, and put them in an oven till they have done making a Noise, then take them out and wipe them well from the

green froth that is upon them, and bruise them shels and all in a Stone Mortar, then take a Quart of Earthworms, scowre them with salt, slit them, and wash well with water from their filth, and in a stone Mortar beat them in pieces, then lay in the bottom of your distilled pot Angelica two handfuls, and two handfuls of Celandine Bearsfoot, Agrimony, red Dock roots, Bark of Barberries, Betony wood Sorrel of each two handfuls, Rue one handful; then lay the Snails and Worms on top of the hearbs and flowers, then pour on three Gallons of the Strongest Ale, and let it stand all night, in the morning put in three ounces of Cloves beaten, sixpennyworth of beaten Saffron, and on the top of them six ounces of shaved Hartshorne, then set on the Limbeck, and close it with paste and so receive the water by pintes, which will be nine in all, the first is the strongest, whereof take in the morning two spoonfuls in four spoonfuls of small Beer, the like in the Afternoon."[1]

Snails were also used topically for rickets. One remedy suggested rubbing snail liquid on the child's joints in front of a warm fire both morning and night. This remedy was known to work in a week's time. Scratching the child's gums with an osprey bone was recommended for teething pain. Most likely this more frequently caused infection than relief of pain.

Children of the 1600s were taught to fear death and work towards purity and heavenly reward. Reading lessons were taught from scripture with these principles in mind. There were no children's books and it was a parent's duty to instill the strict teachings of the Bible as a way of life. By today's standards, these parenting practices may seem harsh but parents were not unloving. They only wanted the best for their children and their children's souls. Though love was not openly demonstrated, it was in a parent's heart and was the basis of a parent's behavior.

From the 1600s to the late 1700s, a child's play was restricted in the name of safety. For example, play in and about water was discouraged as drowning was a leading cause of accidental death. As a precaution, a tithingman had the duty of preventing boys from swimming in Cape Cod's many ponds. This must have been a difficult task as typically a tithingman was responsible for ten families. However, in winter, boys were allowed to skate. Sadly, many fell through the ice and drowned or froze to death. By the end of the 1700s, new games such as playing with marbles and dolls, had become popular.

Though a child's life in these early times may seem bleak by today's standards, families worked together and brothers and sisters enjoyed a full life of family and town activities, especially as Puritan times gave way to the Victorian era. Young girls in the 1800s were taught needle work, knitting, painting on velvet and quilting. Shipping was a large part of the economy in the 1800s and boys often began shipboard life at the age of nine.

During Victorian times, children's lives were filled with more fun and recreation than their parents had enjoyed in their childhood. Parties were held where *blind man's bluff*, and *hunt the thimble* were played. Summer activities included swimming, picnics, sailing, croquet parties and hay-rides. In winter there was ice skating, sleigh racing and ice-boating. Young men and women enjoyed dancing and music. Times were changing from an attitude of Puritan restrictions to Victorian socializing and entertainment. (See Appendix C for descriptions of Blind Man's Bluff and Hunt the Thimble.)

Victorian Recreations
Drawings courtesy of Dover Publications, Inc. NY

Each household was self sustaining. Whether one knew the ways of agriculture or not, families had to plant sufficient produce to feed the entire family. Cattle and other farm animals had to be taken care of. Clearing land for planting was hard labor and every member of the household helped in this task. Sheep had to be sheared and wool spun into yarn. Such chores did not leave much time for leisure. Still, living on Cape Cod had certain advantages over living inland as gifts from the sea were plentiful, and one could always dig for clams or go fishing if crops failed. Fish, especially herring, was so plentiful that one could scoop them up in buckets. Fish that were not eaten were used to fertilize fields.

Taking Care Of Business

Occupations pursued by most people were not as glamorous as shipmaster, shipwright or millwright but they were the jobs that kept families together and towns running. People needed carpenters, tanners, bankers, teachers, and blacksmiths, to name just a few. Some businesses were unique to areas bordering on the sea. One unusual occupation was anchor dragging, the purpose of which was to retrieve lost anchors.

Florence W. Baker describes two small schooners built in 1865 for this purpose:

"Two vessels were used and about 400 fathom of ¾ inch manila rope was attached between the two. The rope was water-soaked until it would sink to the bottom, with a sixty-pound lead on it near each vessel as a sinker. The two vessels would be about one-third of a mile apart and drag that 400 fathom of line on the bottom. In calm weather, the vessels were laid broadside to the tide and, if the wind was favorable, the sails were also used. The anchor fluke or stock would catch the line and stop the vessels. By crossing over the vessels, the one that came in ahead would grapple the other's line. Then, with both lines and crews on one vessel, the line would be hauled in until near the anchor. A heavy messenger was sent down on both lines to prevent the rope from slipping off the anchor. When the anchor was too heavy for the ¾ inch rope, a large hawser was used to raise it. The big rope was put in the yawl to re-sweep the anchor. With three turns around the wooden windlass and long hand-spikes to turn it, the anchor was finally brought to the bow. A heavy tackle from the mast-head was used to hoist the anchor on board the vessel. If there was chain, then that was pulled in, sometimes but a little and sometimes 90 fathom."[2]

In six months, one anchor dragging operation brought up 99 anchors ranging in size from twenty-five to 7,800 pounds. The largest anchor, weighing 7,837 pounds, sold in Boston for $155. Sometimes treasures such as buoys were brought up and these gave added profit to anchor draggers.

Salt marshes were a resource for gardens, animals and houses. Salt thatch was used as fertilizer and for insulation while marsh hay was used to feed cattle during winter. Marsh hay was not used to feed milk cows as it spoiled the milk's taste. Rotting salt thatch replenished soil nutrients and helped ensure productive gardens and farms. Placed against walls, salt thatch blocked cold winter air from entering houses. Today, people still gather salt thatch from marshes for their gardens.

The cooper's shop was a familiar sight and the craft of making barrels was truly an art. Grain and other dry goods as well as liquids needed to be stored. Salted fish, meat, cider, water, beer, rum, whale oil and cranberries were among the many items stored in barrels made by these gifted craftsmen.

THE CAPE COD SOUVENIR

is with us again, it is made in pure silver, only in three sizes, Orange, Tea and Coffee, at reasonable prices. Large quantities of them already sold. For sale by A. L. PUTNAM, Provincetown; C. F. GODFREY, Wareham and Falmouth, J. A. GUYER, Hyannis, R. H. HARRIS, Yarmouthport, E. T. BEARSE, Chatham, ZENO KELLEY, South Yarmouth, E. S. CLARK, Sandwich, J. G. RYDER, Harwichport, GURNEY BROS., Brockton, and F. W. HAYDEN, Middleboro.

1893 Advertisement for Souvenir
Image courtesy of *Yarmouth Register*

As tourists came to visit Cape Cod during the late 1800s, some residents opened their homes to supply lodging and generate much needed cash. Lodging for one week cost five dollars for adults and half this for children. With trains and stages running more frequently, people began to travel for pleasure as well as to visit friends and relatives. Then, as now, artists were attracted by the beautiful scenery and intense lighting Cape Cod offers and came to paint during the summer. This brought additional business to lodging houses and stores all along the cape.

Dry goods stores were important enterprises where flour, grain, groceries and even coal could be purchased. For children, dry goods stores were places to buy candy. These stores served as community post offices and as places for people to meet and visit. This brought potential customers into a store, of benefit to the proprietor as well as the U.S. Postal Service. Here, one would catch up on town news and learn what was happening in the outside world. Mail delivery by stagecoach brings to mind the important role of stage drivers as they delivered both passengers and mail over frequently rough roads in inclement weather.

When the Cape Cod Railroad reached South Yarmouth in 1865, it too created jobs that one does not now often think of, such as station agent and brakeman. Prior to the invention of airbrakes, brakemen set a train's brakes by hand to control speed and stop the train at station platforms. Brakemen played a critical role in ensuring railroad safety. Trains, of course, needed conductors and in those days there was always the job of selling candy, fruit snacks or cigars to passengers as trains chugged on to their destinations.

Freshly caught fish were stored in commercial ice-houses. One cold, difficult task was ice cutting on Cape Cod's frozen ponds in winter. After cutting, the heavy ice blocks were hauled to storage houses. During the early 1900s, Yarmouth businessmen worked to attract industry in order to create jobs and increase the number of year round residents. One such business was the Bay State Freezer Company built in 1916 for use by local fishermen. This facility made its own ice rather than relying on winter freezing.

Located at the old Central Wharf near what is now Wharf Lane in Yarmouth Port, the company was comprised of a five story building containing a 65 ton refrigerator. This was a huge facility with a large wharf allowing ships to dock, load ice or unload fish for processing. An associated ice house had capacity for twenty tons of ice. The Bay State Freezer company had a crew of fisherman and its own weirs to catch and hold fish. Sadly, the company was not long lived. Oliver and Smith describe its demise:

> "The short life of the Bay State Freezer Company was due to a new invention. In 1921, Charles Birdseye developed the quick freeze method of preserving fish, and it quickly revolutionized the deep sea fishing industry. On shore cold storage plants became a thing of the past, as the large fishing vessels could do their own fish processing. A year after Birdseye's invention the company went bankrupt, and the plant was sold. The last vestige of the company, a 100 foot chimney, was torn down in 1966."[3]

The early 1900s was a difficult time for Cape Cod's economy. In 1914 *The Register* reflected the times when it reported that a young man, just starting out in life, should not remain in Yarmouth ... *if he wishes to amount to anything in the world.*

Sometimes skills were combined which provided more business opportunity. During the 1800s, William F. Kenney of South Yarmouth, a jeweler and watchmaker, also took tintype photographs and was in charge of the telegraph office. His shop was complete with fancy chairs and backdrops to create the perfect setting.[i] Mr. Kenney also invented a patent medicine, *Kenney's Speedy Relief*, which sold well.

Other occupations within the community included blacksmith, cobbler, furniture maker and printer. Stagecoaches had to be repaired and painted. But first they had to be built. The Keith Car and Manufacturing Company, started in 1826, built everything from stagecoaches to railroad freight cars.

Town news had to be printed. The *Yarmouth Register* was founded in 1836 by Nathaniel Simpkins. Four years later, Simpkins hired Charles Francis Swift when Swift was only fifteen years old. Ambitious and industrious, Swift began as an apprentice and ten years later, when twenty-five, he owned and operated the business that he then controlled until he died in 1903. To say the least, Swift was an interesting person and was involved in most every aspect of the town.

Cape Cod bogs offered more than just cranberries. Iron ore harvested from bogs in the Bourne-Wareham area was

---

[i] Tintype exposures were necessarily long, roughly a minute, as silver nitrate in collodion was not as light sensitive as today's photographic materials. Consequently, subjects had to remain still for longer than one can normally maintain a smile. To remain still, one relaxed one's face and a small brace held one's head in place. The result of this was that people look very stern in tintype photographs.

While the term tintype is frequently used generically for this type of photography, there were actually two distinct processes. Ambrotype refers to light sensitive silver collodion coated on a glass plate while tintype used iron as the support.

used to make cookware and eating utensils. This was a low grade iron ore deposited by glacial drift. Eventually, people began forming nails from the ore and it was not uncommon for families to have their own simple smelters and forging equipment to make their own nails. Soon the need for nails resulted in formation of manufacturing businesses. The Parker Mills Nail Company, founded in 1819 in Wareham and powered by a waterwheel, later became the Tremont Nail Company. The current factory was completed in 1848 as Tremont nails became known world-wide. As frequently happens, formation of this new company brought ancillary benefit to the community. To this day, the Tremont Nail Company is worth visiting. Now powered by electricity rather than falling water, the old nail making machines are still in use.

Tremont Nail Factory in 2003
Photo courtesy of Edward Weissberger

Paper is an important product for any town and paper manufacturing relied on many diverse companies. The American Metallic Fabric Company of South Yarmouth, started by Samuel Kelly in 1885, manufactured wire belting used in the paper making process. Both Samuel and his brother Seth worked hard to make the company a success. In the beginning, the looms were worked by hand and later by steam engine. Initially the factory produced brass mesh, then mesh made of stainless steel and eventually mesh woven of plastic. The American Metallic Fabric Company stayed in operation as an independent company for ninety years before it was purchased by the Sheaney Bigelow Wireworks.

In 1914, a depressed economy inspired ingenuity as people created new businesses. A group of entrepreneurs in South Yarmouth started a skunk farm to supply pelts to the furrier industry. In the early 1900s, Skunk breeders of Cape Cod surmised that skunk furs would be cheaper than fox furs and would become the latest style. The goal was to increase the sale of products made on Cape Cod and bring economic benefit to the Cape. The skunk fur industry never became a booming business.

In 1945, John Silver, another person interested in profit from skunks, found the way to success. He claimed that skunk oil was a panacea for infirmities from the common cold to croup[j] to lumbago[k]. One swallowed skunk oil by the teaspoon for relief from the croup or massaged it on a sore area as a remedy for sore joints. Skunk oil was a cure *for whatever ailed you*. The demand was so great that John never had to advertise. Some people proclaimed remarkable cures after using skunk oil. One woman claimed that after applying it to her arthritic fingers, she was once again able to thread a needle.

---

[j] The Random House Dictionary of the English Language defines croup *as any condition of the larynx or trachea characterized by a hoarse cough and difficult breathing.*
[k] The Random House Dictionary of the English Language defines lumbago as *pain in the lower or lumbar region of the back or loins.*

Silver produced skunk oil by trapping skunks, skinning them, and then rendering the fat to oil on his kitchen stove. He then strained and bottled it. In 1948, there was a shortage of skunks on Cape Cod and at the age of 80, John walked over 200 miles in search of the furry black and white animal to no avail. A syndicated article entitled, *Depression Hits Skunk Oil Business: Old John Silver Can't Make Scent Now,* reported his plight.[4] People from all over, including Texas and North Dakota, responded by offering to send him oil, asking what he would pay for it.

John Silver with Skunk Oil
Photo courtesy of *The Register*

John Silver continued selling skunk oil until his death in 1956 at age eighty-nine. Fortunately, skunk oil does not have the odor we generally attribute to skunks. Although skunk oil is what made John Silver famous, he also worked as a cobbler, butcher and mason.

The wrecking business, which is not generally thought of as very prestigious, is one that in fact was very important. Cape Cod's treacherous shores and the suddenly changing North Atlantic weather caused innumerable ship wrecks. Lost cargo floating on the seas or deposited on the beaches could be retrieved and, if possible, the ship repaired. Before the late 1800s, lost cargo was free to anyone who could gather it. Needless to say, lost ships and cargo represented enormous financial losses to merchants and captains. The wrecking business helped defer those losses.

Along with wrecking businesses came insurance businesses. During Puritan times there were no insurance businesses as it would have shown a lack of faith to think that *acts of God* should not be taken in stride. But a captain or merchant could loose a ship, cargo and earnings from storms or other disasters. Enterprising individuals gained from the possibility of disasters at sea. Once again, Squire Elisha Doane proved to be an opportunist. Puritan days were long gone and businesses needed financial protection. Squire Doane entered the insurance business and was very successful. He was also owner of a local tavern in Yarmouth and part owner of the packet ship *Eagle Flight*. His tavern was one of the finer establishments and was frequented by gentry.

Taverns were often built near churches. After a long sermon in an unheated church, especially in winter, people gathered at inns or taverns to warm themselves by the fire and catch up on town news. Taverns were places for friendship, information exchange and refreshment. During wartime they were converted into barracks. Today's Old

Yarmouth Inn on Old Kings Highway, Yarmouth Port, was at one time used this way. This tavern, built in 1696, is today a place for fine dinning.

Old Yarmouth Inn built in 1696
Base for stagecoach travel to Chatham and Provincetown
Photo courtesy of Edward Weissberger.

Even in colonial times, drinking alcoholic beverages brought forth many issues. During the 1600s, colonists imported malt and beer and even though they may not have thought much of corn shown to them by Native Indians, they did learn how to make beer from it. A quality control law governed beer making and the price for a pint of beer was not allowed to be more than a penny. In Puritan times it was not prudent to make a profit by selling alcohol.

Taverns were referred to as ordinaries and it is interesting to note that even in 1634 there was a person called *watcher* who was responsible for ensuring that visitors to a tavern did not over indulge.

"At the houses of entertainment called ordinaries into which a stranger went, he was presently followed by one appointed to that office who would thrust himself into his company uninvited, and if he called for more drink the officer thought, in his judgment, he could soberly bear away, he would presently countermand it, and appoint the proportion beyond which he could not get one drop."[5]

Ministers living in visual vicinity of a tavern also kept an eye out for those going in and upon seeing a person enter, noted how long the person stayed. Often the minister went to the tavern to let the person know when he had stayed too long. Even though New England colonists learned to make beer from corn, they did not allow beer to be sold to their Indian neighbors. However, while laws prevented the sale of alcohol to Indians in New England, Indians were free to purchase alcoholic beverages in New York.

Sometimes colonists made mildly fermented drinks that contained less alcohol than common alcoholic beverages such as beer and rum. However, imbibed in sufficient quantity, these fermented beverages had the same effect as alcoholic beverages. One such beverage, called metheglin, was made with water, honey and yeast. A 1633 recipe for metheglin in the language of the times shows that the taste of metheglin must have varied from household to household.

"Take all sorts of Hearbs that are good and wholesome as Balme, Mint, Fennel, Rosemary, Angelica, wilde Thme, Isop, Burnet, Egrimony, and such other as you think fit; some Field Hearbs, but you must not put in too many, but especially Rosemary or any Strong Hearb, lesse than halfe a handfull will serve every sorte, you must boyl your Hearbs & strain them, and let the liquor stand till to Morrow and settle them, take off the clearest Liquor, two Gallons & a halfe to one Gallon of Honey, and that proportion as much as you will make, and let it boyle an houre, and in the boyling skim it very clear, then set it a cooling as you doe Beere, when it is cold take some very good Ale Barme and put into the bottome of the Tubb and a little as they do Beere, keeping back the thicke Setling that lyeth in the bottome of the Vessel that it is cooled in, and when it is all put together cover it with a Cloth and let it worke very neere three dayes, and when you mean to put it up, skim off all the Barme clean, put it up into the Vessel, but you must not stop your Vessel very close in three or four dayes but let it have all the vent, for it will worke and when it is close stopped you must looke very often to it and have a peg in the top to give it vent, when you heare it make a noise as it will do, or else it will breake the Vessell; sometime I make a bag and put in good store of Ginger sliced, some Cloves and Cinnamon and boyl it, it is both good, but Nutmeg & Mace do not well to my Tast."[6]

Even though these ingredients appear quite harmless, one could get drunk on this beverage.

Cape Cod's towns had many taverns; there were seventeen taverns on the Bay side of Yarmouth alone, and drinking eventually became a problem. It wasn't long before prominent citizens joined the Temperance Society, formed in 1817, in order to correct the problem. Some taverns began to lose money and were forced to close. In addition to liquor, the Temperance Society believed that tobacco should be eliminated.

The Temperance Society may have successfully restrained citizens from drinking for awhile, but liquor could not be permanently eliminated from social activity. In 1915, issues of alcohol consumption surfaced once again. Members of the Women's Christian Temperance Union wrote articles published in *The Register* campaigning against the use of alcohol. Laws were passed prohibiting the sale or manufacturing of liquor and finally The National Prohibition Act was passed in 1919. Not everyone was in favor of these laws and with the Prohibition Act came rumrunners.

Along with people from other parts of the Cape, citizens of Yarmouth were involved in smuggling liquor. Heavy traffic on Wharf Lane in conjunction with liquor landing at the pier in Yarmouth Port was noted. A raid on the building of the defunct Bay State Freezer Company in May of 1924 was too late as much of the liquor had already been shipped to Boston. When a ship carrying a cargo of illegal alcohol was wrecked, the evidence drifted ashore. In August, 1926, *The Register* reported:

> "All old soaks have been exuberant this week. With the drifting cases thick as porpoises in a school of mackerel … Power boats putting out from Yarmouth Sunday night came back loaded to the scuppers with crews to match."[7]

Elixirs And Potions: The Business Of Healing

Today's physician is a far cry from doctors of the 1700s. During colonial times there were no colleges to train physicians nor was a medical degree necessary to practice medicine. Anyone interested in medicine and wishing to become a doctor worked as an apprentice alongside an established doctor. As such, the would be physician not only learned treatments of the day but also cared for the doctor's needs, including taking care of his horse and cleaning his house. An apprentice learned to collect herbs and formulate drugs. When he was considered fit to practice on his own, he applied to the court for his license.

Remedies commonly used in the 1700s were certainly different from the highly studied and regulated pharmaceuticals we use today. For example, a remedy given for fever in the 1700s, called *The Water of Life*, was also used as a preventive medicine or tonic to maintain health. Many tonics used in earlier days were made at home and kept on hand for use at any time. A recipe for *The Water of Life* in the language of the times:

"Take Balm leaves and stalks, Betony leaves and flowers, Rosemary, red sage, Taragon, Tormentil leaves, Rossolis and Roses, Carnation, Hyssop, Thyme, red strings that grow upon Savory, red Fennel leaves and root, red Mints, of each a handful; bruise these hearbs and put them in a great earthern pot, & pour on them enough White Wine as will cover them, stop them close, and let them steep for eight or nine days; then put to it Cinnamon, Ginger, Angelica-seeds, Cloves, and Nuttmegs, of each an ounce, a little Saffron, Sugar one pound, Raysins solis stoned one pound, the loyns and legs of an old Coney, a fleshy running Capon, the red flesh of the sinews of a leg of Mutton, four young Chickens, twelve larks, the yolks of twelve Eggs, a loaf of White-bread cut in sops, and two or three ounces of Mithridate or Treacle, & as much Muscadine as will cover them all. Distil al with a moderate fire, and keep the first and second waters by themselves; and when there comes no more by Distilling put more Wine into the pot upon the same stuffe and distil it again, and you shal have another good water. This water strengtheneth the Spirit, Brain, Heart, Liver, and Stomack. Take when need is by itself, or with Ale, Beer, or Wine mingled with Sugar."[8]

Measurement of ingredients during the early 1700s was neither accurate nor precise. Measurements could be described in terms of *the bigth of a walnut, enough to lie on a pen knifes point, the weight of a shilling, a pretty bunch of herbs,* or *take a pretty quantity as often as you please.*[9]

One sickness or discomfort during the 1700s was described as having a *cold stomack.* The recommended remedy for such an ailment was to put either a green piece of turf, grass side down, or a bag of herbs and spices that had been boiled in vinegar on one's stomach. This particular remedy was applied as hot as one could endure. Some remedies included crushed gold, pearls or amber. These jewels were not unusual medicinal ingredients for consumption and melancholy and were used in eye salves as well.

On board ship, the captain dispensed medicine and cared for the sick. Any American ship over 150 tons and with more than ten people on board was required to carry a medicine chest. Even though the captain was not responsible for medical care when on land, he was responsible for dispensing medical treatment while at sea and could only guess at how to proceed or apply written guides. One guide, written by William Hollis, *A Companion to the Medical Chest, with Plain Rules for the Taking of Medicines,* was most likely available to help a captain of the 1800's deal with illness.

Often, many remedies in succession were used to promote cure, sometimes killing the patient. Such an experience is described by Joan Druett in *Hen Frigates.* Captain William Cleveland of the *Zephyr* tried in vein to help a young man on board. The captain had overheard Cornelius Thomson complain of feeling chilly during the night. When questioned about it, the young man, who had celebrated his twenty-first birthday the day before, stated that he felt fine and was planning to go ashore. However, the captain wanted to be sure that good care was given, and to be on the safe side, commenced with the following treatment:

"... Treatment that started with 'a powerful dose of Calomel of Julep,' progressed through a 'dose of castor oil' and several enema injections, to raising blisters 'upon the calf of both legs after soaking them well in hot water,' and culminated with 'a blister on the breast, throat rubbed with linnament & c.' Within hours the poor fellow was out of his head, and by morning he had breathed his last."[10]

Today, our approach to medicine differs from that of earlier times in many and major ways. Students participate in a long, arduous, formal education process, including working beside established physicians, to learn the practical aspects of medicine before they are allowed to practice as physicians. Medicines are prescribed with specific dosages. The business of pharmacology develops and formulates medicines containing specific ingredients, precisely and accurately measured and monitored for quality. Potential drugs are rigorously tested and must meet requirements for efficacy, safety and manufacturability proscribed by the Food and Drug Administration before they may be marketed. Research is constantly undertaken in all medical fields in an effort to both identify new materials and techniques and to improve those already present.

Science and technology have made the *art of medicine* less art and more science. And yet, to a very real extent, the art remains. Modern medicine has improved the quality of life for the elderly and has provided cures for illnesses which were incurable and frequently fatal only a few years ago. When we think of how far medical treatments have advanced, it seems remarkable and yet one cannot help but wonder with a smile whether people a century from now will read about root canal dental surgery, open heart surgery and the popular consumption of over-the-counter vitamins and herbs and express the same astonishment as we who now read of the medical treatments of the past.

Advertisement for Beecham's Pills
Courtesy of *Yarmouth Register*

Cemeteries:
Windows Of The Past

It may seem strange to look at cemeteries as history books, but cemeteries can tell us a great deal about earlier generations and the world they lived in. The perception of death has changed through time and with these changes the rituals of death and how we express grief have also changed.

Attitudes toward death and burial today are quite different from those in earlier centuries. In fact, the word cemetery was not in common use until after the rural-cemetery movement gained influence in the 1830s. The rural-cemetery movement, a new way of thinking of disposition of the dead, came about in 1831 with the founding of Mount Auburn Cemetery. Located in a bucolic rural setting in Cambridge, Massachusetts just outside of Boston, Mount Auburn offered actual lot ownership in a beautiful planned and supervised setting. Prior to this, New England's burial places were known as burial grounds or graveyards.

When death occurred away from home, the deceased was buried in a convenient place near where he or she had died. A marker placed in remembrance at home is known as a cenotaph, meaning that the body was not buried beneath the marker. Because only shovels were used to dig graves, graves were often shallow, sometimes only three feet deep. To protect a new grave site from animals, a large flat stone known as a *wolf stone* was sometimes temporarily placed over the grave.

Although by 1700 there were many known gravestone carvers working in eastern New England, none resided on Cape Cod until early in the nineteenth century because the Cape had no appropriate source of easily carved stone. Stones imported from Boston and Plymouth County in Massachusetts, from several Rhode Island towns and from the carving centers of the Connecticut River Valley are fairly common in Cape Cod burying grounds of the seventeenth and eighteenth centuries. Carvers worked predominately with slate and sandstone. White marble and limestone did not come into common use until early in the 1800s. Most often, the Cape's earliest grave sites were marked with un-carved fieldstones or impermanent wooden post and rail markers. Needless to say, such burial sites can be difficult to distinguish from natural or man-made rock piles. Painted wooden markers, through time, loose their markings and eventually rot away, leaving grave sites devoid of identification.

The epitaph on a marker tells us much about who is buried in that grave site, their town, their beliefs and what the person or the person's relatives wanted us to remember. One of the most common early epitaphs, in use since ancient times, offers a lesson to the casual reader:

> Stop and pause as you pass by
> for as you are now so once was I
> as I am now so you must be,
> prepare for death and follow me.

A less well known answer comes quickly to mind.

> To follow you I'll not consent,
> until I know which way you went!

Sometimes those who died by suicide or from an epidemic disease such as smallpox or cholera were burred outside the established burying grounds. Often a corner of a burial yard was reserved for the poor, blacks, slaves and criminals.

Burials were often held in the evening or even after sunset. In many burying grounds the carved headstone faces west, while the footstone faces east. The body lies between these two markers, facing east, ready to rise up and greet the new day at resurrection. A large horizontal stone raised on pillars is known as a tablestone, or if walled in on all four sides, a box tomb. These more costly markers are an adaptation of the English custom of burying prominent persons within church walls or under the church floor. A person with such a marker is not contained within the box structure but is buried in the ground beneath the tablestone or box tomb. Very early Puritan sites were not regarded as religious or sacred grounds.

Box tomb in Ancient Cemetery, Yarmouth Port
Photo by the author

Prior to the nineteenth century, graveyards and burying grounds were shared by both the living and the dead. Grazing rights were awarded to the highest bidder or given to a townsman who agreed to enclose the burial yard or to keep vegetation in check by grazing his goats or sheep among the stones.

Gravemarkers are historical documents carved in stone. Early Cape stones usually include the name or initials of the deceased along with a date of death and/or age at death, although those who wished, and had the means, could obtain elaborately carved headstones depicting death imps, faces, Father Time and Death, mermaids or elaborate skulls with secondary death symbols. Such embellishments were not uncommon at the end of the 1600s and the beginning of the 1700s.

The rural-cemetery movement began in the mid-1800s when overcrowded and un-cared for burial grounds became a serious concern. More and more land was directed toward residential and commercial use to meet requirements of a growing population just as older burying places filled to capacity. Epidemics of yellow fever and cholera heightened the public's growing anxiety about possible public health issues associated with overcrowded graveyards.

Under the leadership of Jacob Bigelow, a Boston physician and horticulturist, a group of civic leaders purchased land for a spacious and beautifully natural burial site in Cambridge, Massachusetts. Jacob Bigelow envisioned a garden cemetery with unique plantings and walkways for visitors. Mount Auburn Cemetery, the prototype of the rural-cemetery movement, was consecrated in the fall of 1831. Soon large cities and smaller communities all across the nation established similar rural garden cemeteries. In the decades that followed, the term cemetery replaced the often negative images associated with the words burial ground or graveyard. The word *cemetery* derives from the Greek term for dormitory or sleeping place. The new rural cemeteries heralded the public's changing attitude toward death and memorialization.

Much was changing as the 19th century unfolded. A whole new view of death, new social activities, outward expressions of feeling and industrial manufacturing were the beginning signs of this new era. In his description of Mount Auburn Cemetery, David Charles Sloane wrote:

> "It is fitting and natural, then, that the founders of Mount Auburn created a 'garden of graves.' The enormous success of the cemetery and its imitators throughout the nation grew from the public's acceptance of the physical isolation of the dead from the living. The public accepted such a change only within the naturalistic landscape that the founders carefully created from the hills and valleys of the new cemetery. This landscape offered air and light, safety and nature, joy and optimism. By redefining 'the boundary, beyond which the living cannot go nor the dead return', Mount Auburn's planners altered the conventional perspective of the grave and reestablished the cemetery as an important cultural institution within the society."[11]

With the approach of the Victorian era in the mid-1800s, the wording of epitaphs softened from the *body moldering in the ground* to descriptions of one *sleeping peacefully, being at rest* or *going home to heaven.*

Nathaniel Holmes, Cape Cod's first resident carver, moved to the Cape in the early 1800s. Records show that he purchased two acres of land from Edward Phinney in 1809. He continued to buy land and by 1813, when he married Abiah Crocker Davis, his land holdings lay between Hyannis Road and Railroad Avenue, a large tract of land. Although Nathaniel and his wife had nine children, all born in Barnstable, none of them followed him as a carver.

Holme benefited from the Cape's expanding maritime economy during the period from the early 1800s through the Civil War. Records show that Holmes cut an average of thirty-one stones a year, making his annual salary more than school teachers of the time.[1] Carving, along with farming, brought Holmes enough income to support land purchases and improved financial status. Nathaniel Holmes continued carving stones until 1869, seven months before he died at the age of eighty-six. His work is expressed in the form of cherubs, urns and willows, and drapery. Many of his carvings can be seen in Woodside Cemetery in West Yarmouth. Nathaniel Holmes is buried in Barnstable in Cobb's Hill Cemetery surrounded by family members and many of his beautifully carved stones.

Nathaniel Holmes' Home and Workshop
Main Street, Barnstable, MA
Photo courtesy of James Blachowicz

---

[1] An average of twenty carvings a year would have generated the equivalent of a school teacher's salary at that time.

Sally Bearse, 1844, Centerville.
Typical Holmes willow and urn of the 1840s.

Willow and Urn Carving by Nathaniel Holmes
Gravestone located in Centerville, MA
Photo courtesy of James Blachowicz

A town's minister in the 1700s was an important and influential person. Highly educated, he did his best to present sermons that helped the congregation with their spiritual needs. In Yarmouth, Reverend Timothy Alden, a descendent of John Alden of the Mayflower, was such a minister. He was eloquent and known for both strong sermons and thoughtful, imaginative epitaphs. Alden came to his calling in the First Congregational Church of Yarmouth on December 13, 1769. When currency depreciation in 1777 affected his salary to such an extent that he was forced to accept firewood as payment for his services, he found Biblical verse to remind delinquent members of the congregation that wood payment was due.

Epitaphs and information carved on a person's grave marker tell us much about that person, their family and the town they lived in. Reverend Alden wrote many epitaphs and obituaries, some of which are seen on headstones in

Yarmouth Port's Ancient Cemetery. Serving the congregation for fifty-nine years, he was much appreciated for his literary skill and ministry. He continued to write epitaphs until his death at the age of 92. His own epitaph, found on a simple slate stone carved by Nathaniel Holmes with the willow and urn motif in Yarmouth Port's Ancient Cemetery, tells us not only of the person he was, but also how the people of Yarmouth felt about him.

Sacred to the memory
of the
Rev Timothy Alden, A.M.
who was
born 26 Nov ᶜ. O.S. 1736.
graduated at Har. Coll. 1762
ordained at Yarmouth 13 Dec ᶜ 1769
and deceased 13 Nov ᶜ 1828

He was a faithful and devoted pastor
a man of prayer
of a mild, cheerful, amiable disposition
sanctified by grace.
of great humility
exemplary in the various walks
of a long life.
All his hopes rested on the merit of
Jesus Christ
and
his end was peace.
The memory of the just is blessed.

The A.M. located after *Rev. Timothy Alden* shows that he received a Master of Arts degree and was exceptionally well educated. The O.S. refers to *old style*, indicating that the date is based on the Julian calendar. The Julian

calendar, in which the year begins on what today's Gregorian calendar shows as March 25, was used in America before 1752.[m]

Another story is told to us on Captain Benjamine Homer's marker, found in Yarmouth Port's Ancient Cemetery. His is also a simple slate stone with willow and urn motif.

Sacred
To the memory of
Capt. BENJAMINE HOMER
who was shipwrecked and
frozen to death on board
the sch,[r] Huntress on Sandwich
beach Dec'[r] 13th 1825
in his 55th year.
Also LOREN H. HOMER
Son of
Cap,[t] BENJAMINE HOMER
who was lost on board
the Brig Massachusetts on
her passage from Bremen to
Boston Oct,[r] 8th 1823
in his 24th year

Come dearest friends dry up your tears
We hope to meet when Christ appears.

---

[m] The Julian calendar is based on a continuous day count beginning January 1, 4713 BC. Knowing that the Julian calendar's declared year length of 365 ¼ days is incorrect and that this had resulted in a 10 day error by 1582, Pope Gregory XIII introduced the Gregorian calendar in 1582. In 1752, the British Parliament adopted the Gregorian calendar and renamed September 3 as September 14 to account for the 11 day error that had accumulated by that time. (See http://es.rice.edu/ES/humsoc/Galileo/Things/gregorian_calendar.html and www.greenheart.com/billh/gregory.html for excellent historical discussions; see aa.usno.navy.mil/data/docs/JulianDate.html for an on-line date converter.

Bodies of seafarers such as Captain Homer and his son Loren who died far from home were seldom returned for burial. This gravestone in their memory is a cenotaph as the stone does not mark an actual burial site. Rather, it serves only to memorialize the deceased while acknowledging his life and his family's loss.

A cemetery is indeed a history book, telling us how a person died, what they did for a living, and the position they held in society. We not only learn of the people buried in the cemetery, but also of the carvers who spent their lives carving in stone the history of the towns and villages of these people. When we walk in a cemetery, we see more than gravestones and carved memories of loved ones. As visitors, we see the changing seasons and watch the animals scurrying about, and we are reminded that life is eternal.

---

[1] Customs And Fashions In Old New England, Alice Morse Earle, page 6, 7.
[2] Yesterday's Tide, Florence W. Baker, page 174 , 175.
[3] Port On The Bay, John Braginton Smith & Duncan Oliver, page 81, 83.
[4] The Gnome that Lived in Yarmouth, Margaret Milliken, page 81.
[5] Customs And Fashions In Old New England, Alice Morse Earle, page 165.
[6] Customs And Fashions In Old New England, Alice Morse Earle, page 170.
[7] The Town Of Yarmouth, Massachusetts: A History, 1639-1989, Marion Vuilleumier, page 103.
[8] Customs And Fashions In Old New England, Alice Morse Earle, page 337.
[9] Customs And Fashions In Old New England, Alice Morse Earle, page 338.
[10] Hen Frigates, Joan Druett, page 168.
[11] The Last Great Necessity, David Charles Sloan, page 46.

CHAPTER 4:
THE CARVING OF THE CAPE

Cape Cod Weather

The land itself, ever changing, seems to be a metaphor for the changing economy and life on Cape Cod. The storms of Cape Cod are impressive, carving not only the landscape of the shores but also memories in the minds of those who have seen them.

When the Pilgrims arrived in November, 1620, it was weather that kept them from landing on Nauset Beach. Fifteen years later they experienced a storm the likes of which they had never seen. This was the hurricane of August 15, 1635. Trees were twisted and thrown to the ground and the original Aptucxet trading post was destroyed.

Another storm hit the Cape on September 23, 1815, from 10 a.m. to 2 p.m. destroying and carrying away the saltworks on Buzzards Bay. Saltworks from Mashnee Island were later found in Wareham. During this storm the tide rose eight feet higher than normal with the Bay being several feet higher than this. The *Great September Gale*, as it was called, was made famous by a poem written by Oliver Wendell Holmes. (See Appendix D for Holmes' poem.)

There are storms and then there are hurricanes. A brochure written to relieve anxiety among tourists coming to Cape Cod jokingly states: *Hurricane?* *We call them nor'easters ... been having them for 300 years.* If you ask a person who has lived on the Cape which storm was the worst one, they are most likely to say that it was the storm of 1938. This hurricane struck on September 21st with winds of 75 to 90 miles per hour. Wind was not as much of a problem as was danger from storm surge, especially in Buzzards Bay where high tide and storm surge coincided.

When the storm of 1938 hit New York and New England, it sent a tidal wave along the east coast. *The Register* reported that on Cape Cod the south side was hit the hardest with the middle and lower Cape suffering

"... no serious damage other than destruction of property. Boats were driven high and dry, piers demolished. ... At Buzzards Bay, the New Haven railroad tracks were undermined and twisted by the rushing waters."

Woods Hole, Falmouth, all along the shoreline of Buzzards Bay and Buzzards Bay villages suffered extensive property damage. Nearly 600 people lost their lives to this storm; fifteen of those people were on Cape Cod.

Damage to one house and the people in it was devastating. *The Register* reported:

"Mrs. James Lane's, two story wooden house was swept into the Canal at Gray Gables Point and tossed against a huge abutment under the Bourne Bridge. ... Mrs. Lane, Mrs. Wells, Mrs. Needham and grandson were occupants of the house when it was swept away."

A person who had gone to warn the occupants of the coming storm was killed with the others. An employee of Mrs. Lane was also lost to the storm. Their bodies were found near the Buzzards Bay theater. Another employee was swept into Buttermilk Bay, near the Taylor estate, and her body never recovered.

An article in *The Cape Cod Chronicle* tells the story of Albert K. Kendrick, who wrote of his experiences during this storm:

> "... It struck towards dark in full fury. (There was) water up around my barn, boats floating down the road by my house; my house was about 2 feet above it. Houses smashed up, woods below my house full of furniture. Most costly storm in the U.S. She was a corker."

The 1938 Town of Yarmouth, Massachusetts Annual Report, Barnstable County Health Department section reported:

> "... Considerable apprehension was of course aroused by the storm which struck this part of the Country but no particular health problems were caused in this section. All sections effected were watched, water supplies chlorinated where thought necessary etc. The Red Cross was active in its work and gave assistance where ever needed."

Hurricane Carol struck the Cape on August 31, 1954, with winds in excess of 90 miles per hour. Tides were ten feet above normal in some parts of Bourne. Damages on Cape Cod and the Islands were estimated in the millions of dollars. Sixty-eight people on the Eastern Seaboard died from this hurricane.

The Army Corps Of Engineers lowered the Bourne railroad bridge to reduce wind resistance which helped protect the bridge from wind damage but debris in the Canal slammed into the bridge.

The Register related the storm of 1978 to a plastic surgeon:

"While the storm of February 1978 moved across Cape Cod, scientist Graham Giese watched in amazement as the water levels in Provincetown Harbor rose, and rose, and rose.

The two-fisted storm killed power to some 8,000 homes and businesses, caused flooding and took out much of Eastham's Coast Guard Beach and Nauset Spit. When it hit the Cape, winds peaked at 70 and 80 knots and sent record high tides to pound the shorelines and flood marshes and harbors.

The two-day storm changed the Cape's landscape and ecology forever. The huge surf moved tons of sand. Eight cottages perched on the dunes of Coast Guard Beach in Eastham were swept off into the marshes. The Outermost House, the subject of Henry Beston's famous book describing a life of solitude on the Nauset Marsh, was also swept out to sea, as was Conrad Nobili's summer home, which split in two.

In Chatham and Orleans, 90 percent of North Beach was covered with water, and of 38 camps on North Beach in Chatham, eight received some structural or water damage. One of the 12 camps in Orleans was moved from its foundation and one of the nine camps on Monomoy Island was destroyed.

The huge storm, says Giese, 'prepared the Cape for the gradual rise of the sea level that followed.' And more than any single event in decades, it changed the face of this peninsula."[1]

Storms with wind and rain are only one part of Cape Cod's weather history. Droughts, devastating to crops and farm animals, are also a part of the weather story. In the summer of 1749, when agriculture was central to life on the Cape, there was no rain for 108 days. Again, in 1762, no rain occurred for 123 days. There were shortages of grain and food supplies. Those who could afford to, sent to England and the South for supplies. Salt hay alone was not enough to feed cattle and many had to be slaughtered.

Nor'easters, as winter storms are referred to on the Cape, derive their name from the fact that storm winds come from the northeast as they circulate counterclockwise around the center of a low pressure system. These storms can cause equally as much damage as a fall hurricane when they hit the coast in winter months. A nor'easter slammed into the coast from December 26 to 28, 1778. On board the *General Arnold* was a crew of 105 men, mostly from Cape Cod, only 24 of whom survived. Some froze to death when the ship ran aground off Plymouth. Captain James Magee, arriving from Boston, could not get the ship ashore and help could not reach them at sea. People of Cape Cod were devastated by this loss. Items found from the wreck were returned to families of lost crew members. The storm of 1778 became known as the *Magee Storm* and later storms were compared to it.

Erosion at Coast Guard Beach, Eastham, MA
Photo by Barry Donahue; Photo courtesy of *The Register*

In 1816, winter lasted all year. People went hungry when crops failed. Cattle and sheep had to be slaughtered for lack of feed. It snowed every month of the year. June arrived with a nasty cold snap bringing 18 inches of snow to New England while July and August were months of bitter frost. Dry air encouraged forest fires and usually sunny summer days appeared dark as smoke from the fires filled the sky. After such a devastating year, many farmers abandoned life on the Cape and moved west. The strange weather of 1816 was attributed to the April 1815 eruption of the Indonesian volcano Tambora which filled the sky with dust.

Storms associated with this strange weather impacted people around the world. Kim A. Woodbridge, in an article entitled *The Summer of 1816,* states that this storm inspired the writing of famous tales. A group of prominent authors had gathered in Geneva, Switzerland for part of the summer. Included in the group were Mary Shelly, Lord Byron and John Polidori. When a storm struck on June 16th, the group began to read a collection of German ghost stories. Byron, inspired by one of these stories, challenged the group to write a ghost story. Polidori began the original story of *The Vampire.* Mary Shelly, who was having difficulty with her project, continued working on the challenge even after the others had stopped. She even had a dream based on a discussion the group had had regarding manufacture of a human. The dream, according to Woodbridge, was as follows:

"I saw the pale student of unhallowed arts kneeling beside the thing he had put together. I saw the hideous phantasm of a man stretched out, then, on the working of some powerful engine, show signs of life. His success would terrify the artist; he would rush away ... hope that ... this thing ... would subside into dead matter ... he opens his eyes; behold the horrid thing stands at his bedside, opening his curtains ..."[2]

The next morning, Mary knew that she had found her story in what was to be the fourth chapter of *Frankenstein*. The novel was published two years later.

October 2nd and 3rd of 1841 brought a nor'easter that destroyed 60 fishing boats on George's Bank. This storm raged for 30 hours and caused the loss of 200 men. Half of the vessels were owned by Cape Codders which meant that 100 of the men lost were from the Cape. Truro, hardest hit, lost 57 men. Dennis lost 22 men and Yarmouth 10. This storm left more widows and orphans than any other before it. The gale began during the evening of Saturday, October 2nd with hale turning to rain. On Sunday, the winds increased and the storm reached its full fury. Finally, on Tuesday calm began to return.

Fishermen caught at George's Bank had to sail straight into the storm to get home. In order to reach Highland Light, which stood above the Truro bluffs, they had to sail 90 to 120 miles. Vessels in harbors from Provincetown to Chatham were swept on shore. The schooner *The Susan of Boston*, captained by Athens Taylor of Harwich, was destroyed as it sailed from Halifax to Boston. The stern of this schooner was thrown upon the shores near Race Point. *The Susan of Boston* had carried 34 people including a woman and two children, all lost to one of Cape Cod's most devastating storms. (See Appendix E for more about this storm.)

Weather can be spectacular. An August 19, 1896, a thunderstorm generated a giant waterspout at the junction of Vineyard Sound and Nantucket Sound. The funnel cloud was largest on its second of three appearances with a pillar 3,600 feet high. At the cloud base it was 840 feet wide; it was 144 feet wide in the middle and 240 wide at sea level. The cascade was 720 feet wide.

The Great Waterspout of 1896
Photo taken from Cottage City at 1:02 P.M.
Monthly Weather Review, July 1906, p. 356 (NOAA Photo Library)

An article in *The Cape Codder* written by Earle G. Rich tells of a storm known as the *Portland Gale*. Captain Benjamin Hawes, Rich's great uncle, was in this great storm that struck on November 26, 1898. Captain Hawes was known as *Gentleman Ben* because he frequently wore a Prince Albert coat, a Derby hat cocked at a rakish angle and carried a gold headed cane.

> "The early evening of November 26, 1898, found Captain Benjamin Hawes about halfway between the Pollock Rip Lightship off Chatham and his next point of departure, the Bell Buoy marking the extreme eastern end of the Peaked Hill Bars off North Truro. Employed at that time by the Staples Coal Co. of Providence, RI, he was in command of the towboat *Eureka* bound for Boston. ... The holder of a Masters certificate was expected to possess all the needed qualifications required in the performance of his duty as master of his ship."[3]

Rich had a conversation with his great uncle and asked why the captain had not turned back when caught in the gale while towing three coal barges. His great uncle answered:

"There's a lot you don't know yet boy, about towing a string of barges. You have others to think of. I did think of trying to make Nauset Inlet at one time, but gave up the idea knowing my tail barge would never make it. I would much rather have gone down with them then to have been the only survivor."

During this gale, 150 schooners were wrecked on the coast, mostly in the vicinity of Cape Cod, with a loss of one hundred lives. In New York City, removal of snow from the *Portland Gale* required 4,500 men, 3,000 carts and over $100,000.

A 1903 map drawn by The Army Corps of Engineers shows shipwrecks around Cape Cod. In only sixteen years, from 1843 to 1859, approximately five hundred ships were wrecked on the shores of the Cape. Between 1880 and 1903, even though lighthouses had been built along the back side of the Cape, 540 more ships were lost to the sea. When opened in 1914, the Cape Cod Canal helped captains avoid the dangerous areas, greatly decreasing the frequency of shipwrecks and loss of life.

Cape Cod has had its share of storms, droughts and freezing cold winters. It is an area which can on one day be a paradise with beautiful sandy beaches and on another day have debris of shipwrecks strewn along those very same beaches.

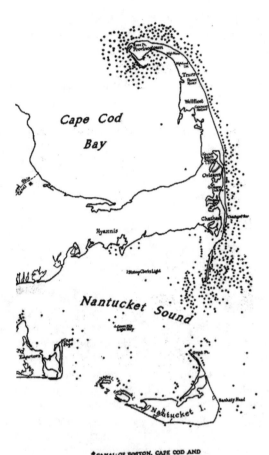

Shipwrecks in Cape Cod Waters
Locations of about 1100 wrecks from 1880 to July 30, 1914
Map courtesy of the U.S. Army Corp of Engineers.

People who live here do all that is possible to rescue those stranded by weather. In the winter of 1873, a total of 75 fishing vessels rounding the Cape were hit by freezing weather. Fifty of the ships were frozen in the ice and blown into Barnstable Bay, now known as Cape Cod Bay, where they remained stranded from February 3rd to March 6th. An article in the *Cape Cod Standard-Times* reported:

> "Volunteers pushed dories over the ice to Provincetown for coal and provisions. Men walked over the ice from the vessels all the way from Provincetown to Sandwich. The cold was so intense, the sailors coming ashore tunneled under salt hay stacks to keep from freezing to death. Today it's hard to imagine Cape Cod Bay covered by thick ice. Walking the roughly 25 miles from Provincetown to Sandwich across exposed, rough ice with strong, cold winds was no easy feat."

The story of Captain Driscoll, then a crew member of one of the ships, tells of the effort.

> "... The date was 1873 when he and 100 other seamen found themselves and their boats frozen solid in an ice pack which reached from Provincetown to Plymouth. There was no telling when the ships would be freed. Fuel was exhausted and food was running out fast. Mr. Driscoll, then a young crew member just recently over from Ireland where he had been born in the Port of Old Kinsale, became the hero of the ice blockade by his forays to keep crew members alive by bringing food to the ships from the mainland. On several occasions before the ships were finally abandoned, he made trips to Provincetown, to Wellfleet and Orleans, bringing all he could carry or drag over the rough ice. The work was hard, the distance long, and the prospects of getting out of the ice pack looked slim, so finally, rather than battle Winter weather any longer, the captains and crews of the many ships abandoned them where they were and made their way to the mainland on foot, carrying with them their belongings."[4]

Mr. Driscoll liked Sandwich so much that he said he would someday return. Ten years later, as captain of the

Lockwood Dredge, which worked on one of the early attempts to build the Cape Cod Canal, he fulfilled his promise. Although dredging of the canal failed, Captain Driscoll and his wife remained in Sandwich. Eventually, at 84 years old, he saw the canal completed and watched canal traffic for many years from his home.

The Chatham Break

Recently, a winter nor'easter made it possible for current visitors to watch and track the carving of the Chatham shoreline. The Chatham lighthouse area has long been a lovely and popular vista for residents and tourists alike. Across the street from the lighthouse is a parking area that overlooks one of the most spectacular sights of Cape Cod, a scene that today looks much different from how it looked in the early 1980s.

In January, 1987, a nor'easter ripped through the lower end of Nauset Beach, the barrier that had effectively protected the Chatham lighthouse beach area from Atlantic storms. With this storm, the Atlantic ocean and its storms gained direct access to the Chatham lighthouse beach, the high bluff and the houses built on the bluff. In 1991, another storm, humorously known as the *No Name Storm*, enlarged this break, thereby further increasing access by the sea and increasing the rate of destructive erosion. The *Chatham Break* has been a constant source of amazement to those interested in how rapidly nature can change our environment.

Winter storms first eroded the beach and then began removing the bluff. Houses along the shore between Holway Street and Andrew Harding Lane collapsed into the sea. One could walk the beach and find bricks and construction materials from what had once been lovely homes. Roughly a third of the parking lot was destroyed and the tennis court to the south had to be rebuilt. But if Nature can take something away, it can also give something in return. Storms move sand from one area to another and now the lighthouse beach is more spectacular than it was prior to the 1987 storm. Stretching in a wide arc toward Monomoy Island, this beach has taken years to grow to its present shape and size. It certainly does not look the same as it did before January, 1987, and it is certain that it will not look as is does now in years to come.

Early Chatham Break
Photo by the author

Chatham Break Recovers – January, 2003
Both photos looking Southeast toward Monomoy Island
Photo courtesy of Edward Weissberger

Erosion

During winter storms, sand is shifted and areas such as Monomoy grow, sometimes at an amazing rate. Paul Schneider describes the changing landscape of Cape Cod:

"Past Truro the forearm of land trends more north-south than it does east-west, so the winter northeasters typically push the sand from there in the direction of Nauset Beach and Monomoy. Monomoy grows even faster than Race Point, and has been known to grow by as much as 175 feet in a year. Sometimes Monomoy is one island, sometimes it's two or more. Sometimes it's connected to the Chatham strip. In the 1850s there was a harbor on Monomoy, called the Powder Hole, big enough to shelter forty ships. The sand closed it off from the sea, and it is now a lake."[5]

Erosion of the Cape is an ever-changing process and is a concern to all who have come and stayed to enjoy the Cape's wonderful beaches. Residents with homes well inland often joke about eventually owning ocean front property. Said jokingly, the statement is sometimes followed by a knowing, nervous laugh. After all, Cape Cod is nothing but a large sand deposit jutting into the North Atlantic and sand does shift from place to place.

"During one week in 1961, 450 feet of Madaket, on Nantucket, washed away. During one decade, the 1870s, the Chatham Twin Lights went from being a healthy 228 feet back from the cliff to 27 inches from the precipice, until finally one went over the brink. By the time the second light went over in 1881, a new light was in place farther back from the edge and the erosion had slowed, at least temporarily. A new opening through Chatham's barrier beach forms roughly every 140 years and then slowly migrates south, until finally the passage of waters out of Pleasant Bay becomes too constricted and the process begins anew."[6]

In the 1600s, Billingsgate Island at the southwestern entrance to Wellfleet harbor was sixty acres of dry land. By the 1940s it had dwindled to a sand bar. Today it's an island at low tide and a shoal at high tide. Geologists speculate that by the year 6001, Cape Cod may not even exist.

Some people believe that building *jetties* will give the Cape a longer life. In the 1930s, people working in the public sector tried to control erosion by building sea walls. *The Register* reported:

> "Whether built by the U.S. Army Corps of Engineers, the WPA, the state, or private owners, the rock piles have, since the 1930s, been forcing sand upstream of them to build up and downstream of them to scour away – at times fulfilling their erosion control mission, but more often simply rearranging our coastline, building up certain beaches at the expense of others. Probably more than any other single construction, this effort to halt erosion had far reaching consequences. And no matter which side prevails in the continuing, acrimonious debate about use of man-made erosion-control structures, they have in this century altered our coastline forever."[7]

For those living along Cape Cod's shoreline, erosion presents an on-going struggle. Cape residents understand and somewhat accept that diminishing land is a way of life. On Nantucket, the Veterans of Foreign Wars had to face this Cape Cod fact of life sooner than expected. The bluff at the end of Tom Nevers Road was being eaten away by wave action. Arnold Paterson and Jim Richard told the story as they stood at the end of the bluff 30 feet above the water:

"We knew the time was coming, we just didn't think it would get here so fast." The Veterans of Foreign Wars building was once where they now stood until erosion caught up with the men of POST No. 8608. "... They packed their valuables into the trailer of an old semi, and razed the building just before the sea could claim it. Seven years ago, nearly 140 feet of solid earth - roughly half the length of a football field - separated the post from the edge and the pounding surf below. That has all vanished now, dispatched in a slow daily concession or ripped away in thick blocks during storms."[8]

When the Veterans signed the building lease in 1977, they thought they would be there for a long time. They were surprised that the land disappeared so fast. In August, 2001, the Woods Hole Oceanographic Institution reported that the effect of erosion causes some areas to lose an average of ten or more feet per year.

Saviors Of The Sea

Shipwrecks and Cape Cod have been together since Europeans first began sailing along the Cape's shores. The Cape's shallow sand bars present ships their greatest danger, as it is here that ships are grounded during storms. Once grounded, pounding surf and wind break ships apart as though they were toy models.

Because many storms on Cape Cod come up suddenly, because the shoreline is so treacherous and because the arm of the Cape stretches twenty-five miles into the ocean, this changing land can be heaven or demon to mariners. For shipping, the Cape's location and protected bays are wonderful, but its location combined with *nor'easters* raises havoc. The Cape has been the location of more than 3,000 shipwrecks in 300 years. One thousand of these occurred between Truro and Wellfleet. During winters of the early 1800s, there was an average of two wrecks every month.

From the time Cape Cod was first settled by Europeans, there has been some type of rescue service for the captains and crews of stranded ships. Until 1872, rescue service was given by volunteers on an informal basis and was not available full time. Full time, federally organized life savers were called *Guardians of the Ocean Graveyard* and were in service on Cape Cod as part of the U.S. Life-Saving Service from 1872 until 1915, when the service was incorporated into the newly formed U.S. Coast Guard. Life-saving was and remains a dangerous business as is made clear by the life saver's motto: *You have to go, but you don't have to come back.*

The first organized life-saving service, the *Massachusetts Humane Society,* began working in 1785 in Boston Harbor and in the 1800s shelters were established on Cape Cod where shipwreck survivors were given shelter and food. Because Humane Society life savers were unpaid volunteers, they were unable to provide constant service. In addition, equipment used by rescuers was not always adequate for the job. Congress tried to help by funding the Humane Society in 1845. In 1872, federally constructed and staffed lifesaving stations initiated the U.S. Life-Saving Service as a department of the Department of Treasury.

Located on Race Point, Highlands, Peaked Hill Bars, Pamet, Cahoon's Hollow, Nauset, Orleans, Chatham, and Monomoy Point, Cape Cod had nine rescue stations. Each station had a crew of six surfmen and a captain, or keeper. Sometimes the work was endlessly boring and other times it was difficult, terrifying, and exhausting.

Lifesaving Station
Cape Cod National Seashore Salt Pond Visitor Center
Photo courtesy of Edward Weissberger

While patrolling beaches, a surfman carried a wooden shingle in front of his face to keep sand from blowing into his eyes. To verify completion of a patrol, surfmen coming from opposite directions met at a small house located halfway between stations and exchanged metal tags or punched a time clock. When a surfman spotted a ship in distress, he ignited a flare to signal the stranded ship that help would be coming and to alert the station crew of the situation. The alarm call was *Ship Ashore*!

Equipment was pulled to the beach by hand or horse-drawn cart and the keeper gave the order of when and where to launch a surfboat. These twenty-five foot wooden boats weighed 700 to 1000 pounds and carried six oarsmen in addition to the keeper who manned the rudder. Because only five victims could be rescued at a time, these small boats often had to return to the wrecked vessel again and again.

The story of the *Wadena* rescue effort on March 17, 1902, is still told. It is one of the rare times that the U.S Life-Saving Service did not succeed in bringing back the victims of a stranded ship. Captain Marshall Eldredge, keeper of the Monomoy Station, had walked three miles on the beach when he saw a distress flag flying from a barge stranded off Monomoy Point.

Wreckers had returned to the schooner-barge *Wadena* following her grounding and a successful crew rescue on March 11. Their intention was to remove *Wadena's* cargo of coal in preparation for re-floating and salvage. On March 16, a northeast gale struck, stranding five of the wreckers who had not returned to shore. Keeper Eldredge and his life-saving crew began a rescue. They reached the *Wadena* and pulled the five men into their small surfboat. However, the last man aboard fell and broke a rower's seat. All the wreckers were crowded into the bottom of the boat as the lifesavers began rowing back to shore. When a wave hit, pouring water into the boat, the wreckers panicked, stood up, and threw their arms around the necks of the surfmen, preventing them from using their oars. The small boat overturned, throwing all on board into the sea. Twice they righted the boat but each time it again overturned. Finally, only Seth Ellis, the number two surfman, remained holding onto the boat; all others were lost to the sea.

The ending of Seth Ellis' report describes the tragedy:

> "By the time the overturned boat had drifted down ... [near] the barge Fitzpatrick, which was also stranded, [and] I waved my hand as a signal for help. I soon saw those on the barge fling a dory over the side ... But could see nothing ... until it hove into sight...with...brave Captain Elmer F. Mayo. He ran the dory alongside of me, and with his help I got into the boat.

To land in the dory through the surf was a perilous undertaking, but Mayo, who is a skilled boatman, carefully picked his way over the rips and headed his little boat for the shore.

Surfman Bloomer of our station ... when he saw Captain Mayo ... ran down into the surf, seized the little boat, and helped Captain Mayo to land safely.

Bloomer was told of the terrible tragedy by Captain Mayo, as I was unable to speak at the time. As I have often said, 'If the persons we took off the barge had kept quiet as we told them to, all hands would have landed safely.'"[9]

Sometimes storms were so severe that it was too treacherous to launch rescue boats. In these cases, a breeches buoy was used. This buoy consisted of a pair of canvas breeches fastened inside a life ring that was suspended from a life line and pulley system strung between the stranded ship and shore.

Breeches Buoy
Cape Cod National Seashore Salt Pond Visitor Center
Photo courtesy of Edward Weissberger

Rigging a breeches buoy was no small feat. A small cannon called a Lyle gun fired a lightweight line from shore to ship. Crewmen of the stranded ship pulled the line onboard along with instructions, paddle, block and pulley, heavier hawser line, and continuous whip lines attached to it. At the same time, surfmen erected a twelve foot wooden crotch that suspended the hawser line and breeches buoy above the surf. They also buried an anchor in the sand to hold the crotch in place. Rigging all of this equipment was expected to take no more than five minutes. Only after everything was in place could one victim at a time, sitting in the breeches buoy, be rescued as the buoy was pulled to shore and then pulled back to the stranded ship for the next rescue.

Lyle Gun and Projectile
Cape Cod National Seashore Salt Pond Visitor Center
Photo courtesy of Edward Weissberger

During summer, when fewer storms occurred, surfmen were released from duty, leaving only the keeper to patrol the shore. Today, a demonstration of a breeches buoy drill is given weekly during summer months by National Seashore Rangers at Race Point, Provincetown.

When the Cape Cod Canal began service in 1914, the incidence of shipwrecks was dramatically reduced as ships no longer had to ply the treacherous waters around the Cape. Introduction of ship-to-shore radio equipment and improved weather forecasting also helped in reducing disasters at sea. Finally it was possible to discontinue the U.S. Live Saving Service as an independent department and the service was incorporated into the U.S. Coast Guard.

Humane Society volunteers and the U.S Life-Saving Service will never be forgotten. Now it is the U.S. Coast Guard, formed in 1915, that undertakes the dangerous duty of rescuing stranded mariners. One could call the basket lowered from helicopters during today's rescues a modern form of the breeches buoy. As was true in earlier times, brave rescuers still put their own lives in danger to save those who are stranded at sea in a raging storm.

(See Appendix E for significant Cape Cod weather events.)

---

[1] The Register, The Moments That Mattered, December 30, 1999, The Upper Cape Codder, article.

[2] The Summer of 1816, Kim A. Woodbridge, June 26, 2001, The HTML Writers Guild, W3C XHTML 1.0.

[3] The Hero Of The Famous Portland Gale, Earle G. Rich, The Cape Codder, March 5, 1970.

[4] This Cold Snap Tough, But 1873 Was Tougher, Mrs. William R. Hendy Jr., Cape Cod Standard-Times, January, 1961.

[5] The Enduring Shore, Paul Schneider, page 86.

[6] The Enduring Shore, Paul Schneider, page 87.

[7] The Register, The Moments That Mattered, Changing Our Coast Forever, December 30, 1999, The Upper Cape Codder, article..

[8] Cape Cod Times, Trevor Maxwell, March 10, 2002, article.

[9] Sea Stories Of Cape Cod and the Islands, Admont Gulick Clark, page 141

CHAPTER 5:
SOLDIERS OF CAPE COD

Wars have been a fact of life through time and the history and strategy of them have been recorded in many texts. However, it is a soldier's story that tells us the reality of war. Soldiers' experiences are the heart of war. Through their words we feel the soldiers' fear, excitement and loneliness. Through their eyes we see how courage and dedication to their country have given us the lives we live today.

Revolutionary War

In 1773, problems brewing over import taxation in the Colonies came to a head when Boston's governor, Thomas Hutchinson, insisted that tea coming into port not be halted or sent back as had been done in other ports. Emotions exploded and on December 16, 1773, the people of Boston dumped 342 chests of tea into the harbor. In March, 1774, Britain's Parliament closed the port of Boston to all trade and in May implemented the Coercive Acts, restricting Massachusetts' government.

Parliament's idea of setting Massachusetts as an example to the other colonies backfired and in September, 1774, the First Continental Congress met in Philadelphia to protest the Coercive Acts and to organize a new non-importation movement. By this time Massachusetts had a

new governor, General Thomas Gage, a man reported to have had a calm and gentle nature.

Gage tried to solve increasing colonial unrest by working with colonists and strove to deal with many resolutions put forth by the Massachusetts Provincial Congress. However, upon learning of armaments being stored by colonists in Concord, only a twenty-one mile march from Boston, he sent British troops to destroy them. Soldiers crossed the Charles River into Cambridge and continued marching northwest. On Lexington Commons they encountered a local militia and shots were fired. At Concord they encountered even more persistent resistance and retreated under fire. A revolution that would dramatically alter the course of world history had begun.

The Otis Family

Does politics run in families? In the case of the Otis family it does. James Otis, born in 1725 in Barnstable, Massachusetts, became a lawyer in Boston. He was a passionate man, willing to speak his mind. He did so in 1761 when responding to the *Writs of Assistance*, general warrants which allowed officials to search for smuggled goods on any premise. Smuggling was common in the colonies as a way to avoid taxation on imported goods. At a time when the legality of such searches was being questioned, James Otis was Advocate-General and as such was asked to defend the legality of the *writs*. Rather than doing so, he resigned.

When Otis was retained as counsel by British merchants to oppose the *writs* before the Superior Court of Massachusetts, he declined payment and used the opportunity to deliver a five hour speech. Rather than explaining why he had declined payment for services, he raised a fundamental issue pertaining to the rights of government. Basing his argument on rights guaranteed by British common law, he asked to what extent it was appropriate or necessary to obey laws passed by those who were not obliged to obey them? Later, John Adams who as a young man had heard Otis' speech, declared that it was on this day that *the child independence was born.*

In 1764, Otis was made head of the Massachusetts Committee of Correspondence. He continued defending colonial positions and was an active member of the Stamp Act Congress which submitted petitions of complaint to Parliament pertaining to the Stamp Act. This act imposed a tax on the people in order to raise revenue. The British ministry embossed stamps of varying value on sheets of paper and sold the paper to colonists for use as legal documents, newspapers and pamphlets. Since a document without a stamp had no legal standing, colonists were obliged to buy stamps and pay the tax.

People began rallying against the tax and even went so far as to physically attack neighbors who distributed stamps. It was widely believed that those distributing stamps benefited from the tax and therefore were not to be trusted. As Otis' influence increased, conservatives began to despise him. Still, this did not deter him from helping Samuel Adams draft a letter to the other colonies denouncing the Townshend Acts in 1767. Charles Townshend had proposed import duties on glass, lead, paints, paper, and tea similar to those on sugar and molasses.

Samuel Adams and the fight for freedom lost the benefit and help of James Otis in 1769 due to a strange and unfortunate incident. When Mr. Robinson, a customs commissioner, misrepresented Otis in England, Otis verbally attacked him in a Boston newspaper. Otis' response enraged the commissioner and when he saw Otis in a local coffee house, he attempted to pull his nose. A ruckus ensued which ended when Otis was struck severely on his head with a heavy cane. James Otis never fully recovered from the injury and was no longer able to be of service to his cause. He lived disabled until May of 1782, when he was struck by lightning and killed while standing in the doorway of a friend's house.

Active political life in the Otis family did not end with James' injury. James had a younger sister, Mercy, born on September 25, 1728, also in Barnstable. During colonial times women were not generally allowed to participate in political matters. However, being an intelligent woman dedicated to the American cause, Mercy Otis expressed her political statements through poetry, songs and a three volume book, *History of the Revolutionary War*, written in 1805. When her brother James was recognized as a pre-revolution leader, she acted as counselor to him and his friends, Samuel Adams and John Hancock.

In 1754, at the age of twenty-six, Mercy Otis married James Warren from Plymouth, Massachusetts. Warren had graduated from Harvard in 1745 and in 1757 followed in his father's footsteps of public service as Plymouth County sheriff. In 1766, he began a twelve year term on the Massachusetts General Court. Warren was an active patriot and spoke openly against British rule. When his friend and fellow patriot Dr. Joseph Warren died at the Battle of Bunker Hill, James Warren succeeded him as president of the Massachusetts Provisional Congress.

James, writing to Mercy from his post in Watertown on June 18, 1775, recounted the events of the Bunker Hill battle and the death of his friend:

My Dear Mercy,
The Extraordinary Nature of the Events which have taken place in the last 48 Hours has Interrupted that steady & only Intercourse which the situation of publick affairs allows me. the Night before last our Troops possesd themselves of a Hill in Charlestown & had time only to heave up an Imperfect Breastwork the regular Troops from the Batterys in Boston & two Men of War in the Ferryway began early next Morning a Heavy Fire on them which was Continued till about Noon when they Landed a large number of Troops & after a Stout resistance & great Loss on their side dispossessd. our Men, who with the Accumulated disadvantages of being Exposed to the fire of their Cannon & the want of Ammunition & not being supported by fresh Troops were obliged to abandon the Town & retire to our Lines towards Cambridge to which they made a very handsome Addition last Night. with a Savage Barbarity never practised among Civilized Nations they fired & have Utterly destroyed the Town of Charlestown. We have had this day at Dinner another Alarm that they were Advancing on our Lines after having reinforced their Troops with their Horse, &c., & that they were out at Roxbury we Expected this would have been and Important day. they are reinforced but have not Advanced, so things remain at present as they were we have killed many men & have killed & wounded about [six] hundred by the best accounts I can get. Among the first of which to our inexpressible Grief is my Friend Doctor Warren who was killd. it is supposed in the Lines on the Hill at Charlestown in a Manner more Glorious to himself that the fate of Wolf on the plains of Abraham. Many other officers are wounded and some killd. it is Impossible to describe the Confusion in this place, Women & Children flying into the Country, armed Men Going to the field, and wounded Men returning from there fill the Streets. I shant Attempt a description--your Brother borrowed a Gun, &c,

& went among the flying Bullets at Charlestown retd. last Evening 10 o'Clock. The Librarian got a slight wound with a musket Ball in his Hand. Howland has this minute come in with your Letter. The Continental Congress have done & are doing every thing we can wish. Dr. Church recd. Last Evening & Brot. resolutions for assuming Govt. & for supplying provisions & powder, & he tells us tho under the rose that they are contemplating & have perhaps finished the Establishmt. Of the Army & an Emission of money to pay & support them, & he thinks the Operations of yesterday will be more than sufficient to Induce them to recommend the Assumtion of new forms of Govt. to all the Colonies I wish I could be more perticular. I am now in a Committee of Importance. & only steal time to add Sentences seperately. I feel for my Dear Wife least her Apprehensions should hurt her health be not Concerned about me. take care of your Self. you can secure a retreat & have proper Notice in Season. & if you are safe & the Boys I shall be happy fall what will to my Interest. I cant be willing you should come into this part of the Country at present. I will see you as soon as possible can't say when, the Mode of Govt. prescribd. is according to the last Charter. some are quite satisfied with it you know I wishd for a more perfect one, it is now Monday Morning. I hear nothing yet but the roaring of Cannon below. but no Body regards them I need not say that I long to see you. perhaps never more in my life. I shall try hard for it this week I hope your Strawberries are well taken care of & that you have fine feasting on them. Your Brother is waiting for Freeman, who with all his patriotism has left us for 10 days. I have Letters from both Mr Adams & Cushing. I can't Inclose them, because I must answer them when I can get oppt. I am calld. on & must Conclude with my wishes & prayers for your Happiness & with Love to my Boys & regards to Friends Your Aff: Husband,
Jas: Warren S:

Adams is very unwell--the Jaundice to a great degree & his Spirits somewhat depressd. Church hopes he will recover. I hope some of us will survive this Contest. Church has put into my hands A curious lett. full of Interesting Intelligence I wish I could give it to you you may remember to ask me about it & the author. I have shewn it to Coll Otis if he goes before me enquire of him. Your Brother Jem dined with us yesterday behaved well till dinner was almost done & then in the old way got up went off where I know not. has been about Cambridge & Roxbury several days

Adieu.[1]

It is apparent from James Warren's comment, that Mercy's brother, James Otis, was still afflicted from being struck on the head in 1769. After the war, James Warren returned home but was unable to gain election to state office. He died in 1808. Mercy Otis Warren died in Plymouth, Massachusetts on October 19, 1814.

On July 4, 2001, a statue of Mercy Otis Warren, sculpted by David Lewis, was unveiled in front of the Barnstable Superior Court. On October 5, 2002, Mercy Otis Warren was inducted into the National Women's Hall of Fame, a nonprofit organization dedicated to the contributions of women to society. The National Women's Hall of Fame was formed in 1969 in Seneca Falls, New York on the site of the first Women's Rights Convention of 1848.

Enoch Crosby

Another citizen of Cape Cod who influenced the course of the American Revolution was Enoch Crosby. On October 15, 1832, Enoch Crosby, 82 years old, was sworn in before the court of Oyer & Terminer in Putnam County, New York, in order to testify in support of his receiving benefits for his service to the United States. He told an interesting story.

Enoch Crosby, born in 1750 in Harwich, Massachusetts, was the great spy of the Revolutionary War. In August, 1776, Crosby was assigned to the regiment of Colonel Sworthaut. However, Colonel Sworthaut's company had left Fredericksburgh, now Carmel in Putnam County, located in northeastern Connecticut, and was on its way to Westchester County, forcing Crosby to attempt to join his company on his own.

While traveling to join his company, Crosby came upon a stranger, named Bunker, who asked where he was going. Suspecting that Bunker thought he was going to join the British, Crosby asked him for safe directions to the British lines. Bunker told him that there was a loyalist company forming in the vicinity and encouraged him to join it. Crosby then informed Bunker that he was unwilling to wait until the company was ready to march and that he would go forward on his own. He continued walking until darkness set in and then spent the night at the home of Esquire Young who was a member of the Committee of Safety for Westchester county. While there, he told Young of his conversation with Bunker. Upon hearing what Crosby had learned, Young requested that Crosby go with him to report to the committee. Crosby did as requested and from that time on was assigned the role of secret agent. Colonel Sworthaut soon received a letter stating that Enoch Crosby would not join his regiment.

Crosby was introduced to Captain Townsend who was apprised of Crosby's new role. He joined Captain Townsend, posing as a prisoner. That evening, Crosby *escaped* and went to Mr. Bunker's house saying that he had escaped from Townsend's camp and was looking for protection. The next morning Bunker introduced him as a good loyalist to several men in his company. Crosby stayed with these men for a short time. Eventually he returned to Esquire Young's home, five miles away, where he reported on the loyalist company and its location to Young and Captain Townsend. He then made his way back to Bunker's home where he rejoined the loyalist group.

The next day, Crosby and about thirty others of the loyalist company were captured and taken to White Plains. Later they were taken to Fishkill in Dutchess County where Captain Townsend took charge of the prisoners. Crosby remained there with the others, guarded by rangers commanded by Captain Clark. After being interred for about a week, he was freed on bail in order to maintain his cover.

Enoch Crosby was then given a secret pass and an assignment to go to the house of Nicholas Brawer near the mouth of Wappingers creek. Brawer took Crosby across the Hudson river whereupon Crosby made his way to the house of John Russell, ten miles away. Under guise as an employee, Crosby gathered more loyalist information and reported to his company in Fishkill after ten days.

Eventually, Crosby joined a thirty man company commanded by an English officer named Captain Robinson. After a week's time, the company began a march from Ulster County to Bush Carricks, resting in a barn for the night. By morning the barn was surrounded by American troops and all were taken prisoner. Once again, Crosby was a prisoner of war, held by his own forces. Robinson's company was taken to Fishkill and confined in a stone church along with other prisoners. After one night, the Americans removed Crosby from the church as it seemed unsafe for him to remain with British prisoners. He was instructed to leave Fishkill but remain available for further duty. Within a few weeks he was sent a horse and instructed to go to a place named Maloonscack where he met a Tory named Hazard Wilcox.

Because he received no information from Wilcox, Crosby went to Pawling in Dutchess County and while there learned that a British Captain named Sheldon would lead a march. He reported this to his contacts.

Crosby had been working successfully as a spy for a year when he was taken prisoner for the fourth time, again by Americans. When the order came for the prisoners to be tied together, Crosby claimed he was too lame to travel. The captain in charge, aware of Crosby's role, took him to prison on his horse. When they reached Fishkill, Crosby was again released.

After reporting to the Committee of Safety, Enoch Crosby was released from duty as a secret agent and allowed to return to his home. He enlisted two more times for regular duty and eventually settled in New York State's Putnam County without ever having received a formal discharge.

Enoch Crosby's life was so remarkable that James Fenimore Cooper made him the model for his novel, *The Spy,* written in 1821. In 1827, Enoch Crosby attended the play based on this best-selling novel and his own life.

Civil War

Cape Cod and the whole United States experienced dramatic change in the mid-1800s. Not only were there social and political changes but economic changes as well. It was during this time that the Civil War altered the very nature of our country forever. This war separated families

and friends and brought suffering and death to more soldiers than any previous war.

As the middle 1800s arrived, Cape Cod's economy was strong and its people were prosperous. The shipping industry was booming. Saltworks were a leading industry and the fishing industry was productive. Nevertheless, although commerce was thriving, social and political unrest and dissatisfaction were becoming increasingly strong as people expressed differences of opinion about slavery. Some people even left their church when it either supported slavery or accepted members who did.

The historian Henry C. Kittredge wrote:

> "The most prosperous and active years in the history of the Cape – those from the thirties to the fifties – were not occupied exclusively with building bridges and dikes, erecting factories and salt works, drying codfish, and greeting deep-water shipmasters on their return from the antipodes. Such activities were marred by a less desirable manifestation of energy – schism in the churches. Not that schism was anything new or particularly undesirable. Usually it is an indication that progress is in the offing. Furthermore, this particular rift in the ranks of the church was brought about by a sufficiently righteous motive on the part of those who left the fold. They refused to support any longer a church which preached Christianity on the one hand and on the other received into membership men who tolerated slavery. Those who broke away were called 'Come-Outers' (or 'Comers Out'), a name which was not restricted to these groups of Abolitionists, but had been given pretty generally to all who for any reason had seceded from an established church."[2]

Come-Outers did not cause difficulties within the towns as they were merely standing up for what they believed was right across a variety of subjects. However, those from areas other than Cape Cod who specifically agitated against slavery did cause problems. When they came to the Cape they stirred up strongly held beliefs and escalated problems that were already brewing.

Kittredge described an incident that occurred in 1848 which caused considerable unrest:

> "A report had been spread in anti-slavery circles in Boston that a Harwich coasting captain, whose name is not recorded, had taken one hundred dollars from a Negro in Norfolk to bring him and a friend North on his schooner, and had then seized him and had him advertised as a runaway slave. Such indignation was aroused by this outrage that a group of distinguished Boston Abolitionists visited Harwich and held and indignation meeting. Among them were Parker Pillsbury, Stephen Foster, and Lucy Stone. No building in Harwich, or for that matter on the Cape, was big enough to hold the crowd that assembled; men and women poured in from the neighboring towns until, according to one estimate, three thousand had gathered in the grove where the convention was held."[3]

Slavery brought forth strongly held differences of opinion and fighting sometimes ensued following emotional speeches. Still, as a general rule, Cape seafaring abolitionists mostly stood back from strong involvement on the slavery issue. Others who were not as tolerant spoke openly against the *Come-Outers* calling them traitors who had no understanding of the view that Southerners were within their rights to live as they wished.

Other Cape residents did not stand back from involvement on the slavery issue and some took risks to help slaves achieve freedom. A wealthy Osterville ship owner, George Lovell, smuggled slaves aboard his ship to Cape Cod whereupon they followed the *underground railroad* to the home of either Ezekiel Thacher or Alvin Howes in Barnstable. People such as Thacher and Howes took great risks in supporting the *underground railroad* as they were subject to prison sentences and fines if caught.

In order to guard the secrecy of escape routes and protect escaped slaves and those helping them, a code language was used. The *underground railroad* refers to the network of escape routes, places of safety, and those who helped slaves escape to freedom. *Underground* was a reference to the secretive nature of the process as well as the tunnels and cellars used to hide runaway slaves. Escape routes were called *lines* and the slaves escaping were *freight*. Places of safety were called *stations* and helpers were referred to as *conductors*. Lanterns hung on particular hitching posts often signaled which direction to take. Frequently, escaped slaves traveled on Mary Dunn road, running south from Old Kings Highway at the border between Yarmouth and Barnstable, where woods provided shelter and a clearing provided a place where they enjoyed camaraderie and rum.

With the onset of the American Civil War, confusion and differences among residents of Cape Cod regarding slavery quickly abated as people turned to the task of meeting President Lincoln's call to maintain the unity of the republic. Cape Cod responded with loyal dedication. When shots were fired at Fort Sumter in 1861, residents of Yarmouth joined together to support President Lincoln's call for soldiers. On July 3, 1862, a town meeting was held to discuss the salary of volunteer soldiers.

The war profoundly effected the Cape's economy. Only at great risk could sea captains continue trading voyages and fishing captains struggled with a collapsing market. These were difficult economic times for the people of Cape Cod. Captain Forbes tells of his observations while patrolling Cape Cod Bay and the region north toward Boston on July 8, 1861:

> "I have visited Salem, Beverly, Gloucester, Provincetown, Barnstable. ... In all these ports and many others there are hundreds of vessels laying idle and thousands of men, second to none in loyalty, second to none in experience of our Southern Coast, and second to none in all the elements which constitute the accomplished seaman – excepting only a want of knowledge of the art of war....Their fish markets are cut off, and the stock of last season is on hand to a considerable amount, unsold and unsaleable;...At this moment I have in view from my Yacht a hundred sail, more or less, in Provincetown, Wellfleet and Truro laid up for want of work to do."[4]

In spite of severe economic hardships, Cape Cod towns responded to the call to arms with great energy and financial support. Twenty-five hundred men answered the call for soldiers and the sum of half a million dollars was raised in financial support of the war.

"THREE CHEERS FOR THE RED WHITE AND BLUE"

SEAMEN WANTED!

SEAMEN WANTED FOR THE

United States Navy!

WANTED, a large number of able-bodied men for

The Country's Service.

We appeal to

CAPE COD MEN

to come forward.

☞ Good Pay, Glorious Work, and good usage; and all who desire may leave

Half Pay with their Families!

ENLISTMENTS NOW GOING ON!

Seamen's Pay.	—	—	—	—	—	—$18
Ordinary do.,	—	—	—	—	—	— 14
Landsmen's do.	—	—	—	—	—	— 12

and good chance for promotion.
$1,80 per month extra if "grog" is not drawn.

☞ For further information, apply at once to JOSEPH K. BAKER, Jr., Dep'y Collector, West Harwich.

Lieut. E. D. BARNES, Ag't.

Jan. 9, 1862,

GENERAL ORDER.

Civil War Naval Recruitment
Courtesy of *The Register.*

Joseph Eldridge Hamblin

The story of Brevet Major General Joseph Eldridge Hamblin is one of Yarmouth's proudest stories. Born on January 13, 1828, to Benjamin and Hannah Hamblin, he was Yarmouth's first soldier mustered into service. As a young boy, Hamblin divided his time between Yarmouth and Boston and when he enlisted he was working in a mercantile business in New York City. Within two years Joseph Hamblin had achieved the rank of Colonel. He participated in every major battle of the war and when severely wounded at Cedar Creek on October 19, 1864, he refused to leave his battlefield post. This battle was a key Union victory that contributed to Lincoln's re-election and victory.

After his promotion to the rank of Brigadier General, Hamblin returned home to recover from his wounds and then returned to service. His distinguished bravery at Sailor's Creek on April 6, 1865, led to his being brevetted[n] to the rank of Major General. This battle was the last engagement between the Confederate army and the Army of the Potomac prior to the Confederate surrender at Appomattox. Brevet Major General Joseph Eldridge Hamblin mustered out of the army at Washington soon after the war ended as the last Yarmouth soldier mustered out.

After the war, Hamblin returned to New York City where he died on July 3, 1870, of illness contracted during the war. Buried in Yarmouth Port's Woodside Cemetery on Summer Street, Joseph Hamblin is remembered as a gentleman and a leader.

---

[n] The Random House Dictionary of the English Language defines brevet as *a commission promoting a military officer to a higher rank without increase of pay and with limited exercise of the higher rank, often granted as an honor immediately before retirement.*

The Vote

Yarmouth (and Cape Cod) overwhelmingly voted for Lincoln in both 1860 and 1864. **Below**, the local results for 1860 (top) and 1864 (bottom) and the result of the national vote in 1864 (right).

Vote of Barnstable County.

PRESIDENT

	Lincoln.	Breck.	Bell.	Doug.
Barnstable,	364	112	23	13
Brewster,	57	7	43	
Chatham,	96	42	25	
Dennis,	154	19	20	2
Eastham,	66	6	15	
Falmouth,	269	65	39	1
Harwich,	160	19	6	
Orleans,	99	23	45	
Provincetown,	319	26	1	15
Sandwich,	422	41	55	89
Truro,	70	11	1	
Wellfleet,	125	22	7	
Yarmouth,	166	15	9	13
	2367	408	289	133

Below we present the details of the vote :

FOR PRESIDENT.

	Lincoln.	McClellan.
Barnstable,	491	151
Brewster,	143	41
Chatham,	219	106
Dennis,	360	39
Eastham,	81	23
Falmouth,	346	36
Harwich,	370	17
Orleans,	220	24
Provincetown,	494	48
Sandwich,	444	119
Truro,	175	28
Wellfleet,	364	26
Yarmouth,	286	42
	3994	700

In 1860 Lincoln received 2367 votes Breckinridge 408, Bell 289, Douglas 133.

THE PRESIDENTIAL VOTE, 1864.

Triumphant Election

— OF THE —

REPUBLICAN UNION CANDIDATES.

FOR PRESIDENT,

ABRAHAM LINCOLN.

OF ILLINOIS.

FOR VICE PRESIDENT,

ANDREW JOHNSON,

OF TENNESSEE.

We give below the result of the election of last Tuesday, by States, showing the complete and overwhelming success of the Unionists and the triumphant election of LINCOLN and JOHNSON as the next President and Vice President of the United States.

FOR LINCOLN AND JOHNSON.

States.	Electoral votes.
MAINE,	7
NEW HAMPSHIRE,	5
VERMONT,	5
MASSACHUSETTS,	12
RHODE ISLAND,	4
CONNECTICUT,	6
NEW YORK,	33
PENNSYLVANIA,	26
WEST VIRGINIA,	5
OHIO,	21
INDIANA,	13
ILLINOIS,	15
WISCONSIN,	8
MICHIGAN,	8
IOWA,	8
KANSAS,	3
MINNESOTA,	4
MARYLAND,	7
MISSOURI,	11
	201

FOR McCLELLAN & PENDLETON.

NEW JERSEY,	7
KENTUCKY,	11
DELAWARE,	3
	21

DOUBTFUL.

OREGON,	3
CALIFORNIA,	5
NEVADA,	3
	11

Cape Cod's Voting in 1860
Courtesy of *Yarmouth Register*

John J. Ryder

John J. Ryder, born in West Brewster on April 7, 1843, grew up in an area known as the Winslow neighborhood. On August 14, 1862, when he was twenty-one, Ryder left his brother, sister and widowed mother for Washington to fight in the Civil War. With him were Frances W. Penniman, Henry F. Morrison, Nathan A. Gill, Peter Higgins, Thaddeus C. Baker, James Studley and Bangs Baker from Eastham and Orleans.

In letters to his family, Ryder described a soldier's understanding of the war. Some of his descriptions are of battlefield and strategic failures that he believed caused much unnecessary suffering.

"I haven't time now to write of the flagrant errors committed by some of the general officers in command of the different corps by which we suffered our defeat, they have all answered the last roll call -- but my grief and heartache was for the brave men whose lives were sacrificed unnecessarily the afternoon of May 2, when Stonewall Jackson with his 18,000 men was allowed to come down on our wholly unprotected right flank and annihilate it. If our large brigade in which my regiment was, had been allowed to remain where we had been placed, a different story would have been written of that evening attack. But half an hour before the attack came, General Devens ordered our whole brigade away, so we could take no part whatever in the fight. Then the next day half of our army was held in reserve while the other half was closely engaged with the enemy throughout the day with heavy losses thereby. We continually said, 'Why doesn't General Hooker order in the rest of our corps, and use Lee's forces up between us, and end this battle in our favor?'

The sights I saw that day burn in my memory yet. The fires that swept through the woods where our wounded lay helpless – some we carried through the flame and smoke to safety; but oh, the cries of those we couldn't reach! Hundreds perished in that manner."[5]

In other letters, Ryder's writing shows that not all times were frustrating but rather many were filled with great bravery. When thirty marksmen volunteers were asked to enter an open field to distract the Rebel cavalry, men came forward without hesitation, knowing that they would likely be killed or wounded. Stationed ten yards apart in a single line with no protection, they fired upon the enemy in fear that if they were not shot by the Rebels, they would be trampled by their horses. When shooting finally ended, a Union officer rode among the marksmen as fast as he could, telling them to leave the area as quickly as possible as they were the only Northern soldiers in the area. Running as fast as possible, the men safely retreated. Cold and wet, they spent the night shivering and many became ill. Their march to their previous camp was cancelled as Lee's whole army headed toward Maryland and the marksmen were ordered to remain between Lee and Washington.

Ryder wrote of the battle at Gettysburg, fought from July 1st to 3rd, 1863:

"As I think of the thousands who fell in defense of the flag on Gettysburg battlefield, those inspired words of Abraham Lincoln are full of meaning where he says, 'But in a larger sense we cannot dedicate, -- we cannot consecrate, -- we cannot hallow, this ground. The brave men living and dead who struggled here, have consecrated it far above our power to add or detract. The world will little note nor long remember what we say here – but it can never forget what *they did here.*'

"There was so much at stake in the results of this battle on both sides in regard to the success of the Confederacy, that the overwhelming defeat of Lee gave it the name of the High Water Mark of the Southern Confederacy, for from that time their cause continued to decline. History records that General Lee said that after the defeat of his army at Gettysburg he had no hope of the success of the Confederate cause."[6]

On July 4, 1863, the men were sent to the area where Pickett's charge had taken place. In order to remain out of the line of fire, they had to lie down all day. The next day they advanced and took possession of the Rebel's rifle pits. When Ryder reached the pits, he found a rain soaked biscuit and ate it. When he looked around the area, he was shocked to see fifty dead horses in a space of fifty feet and upon looking to the rear he saw a thousand more. Thinking of the loss of human life which had occurred, he watched as burial parties tried to burn the dead horses.

Ryder also wrote of an incident he considered poor strategy in pursuit of General Lee:

"In a few days our army reached a position a few miles from Williamsport, Maryland, at which place General Lee's army was concentrated, the river being too high for him to cross.

As his loss had amounted to 40,000 men, we felt fully able to defeat him and help end the war, but for some unexplainable reason our attack was deferred and Lee was permitted to remain unmolested until the river subsided enough for him to recross into Virginia. Some strange hallucination seemed to have possessed our commanding officers in letting Lee's army retreat when we had him almost in our hands. President Lincoln was greatly disappointed in our failure to attack him.

I have no doubt but General Mead was over cautious, but if either Grant, Sherman or Sheridan had been in command Lee would never have crossed the river unmolested, nor would he have been allowed to cross it at

all, in the opinion of the rank and file – the thinking private soldier of the Army of the Potomac."[7]

As they marched on frozen ground for 140 miles to relieve Burnside at Knoxville, Tennessee, many soldiers wore through the soles of their boots and resorted to untanned cattle skin to protect their feet. Unfortunately, these makeshift shoes only lasted a few days. By the time the marchers reached their destination, they were leaving tracks of blood along the frozen ground. Upon their arrival, they found the Confederates had retreated and within one day had to retrace their steps to obtain food and clothing. The weather was unusually cold and not only were they without shoes, but their trousers were badly torn by bushes and briars. In order to hold their trousers together, they pinned them with thorns.

By June 22, 1864, Ryder's regiment, which was comprised of a thousand officers and men when they departed Massachusetts only two years earlier, had decreased to 170 officers and men. His company had decreased to only twelve men and yet they were still kept on the front lines.

John Ryder was wounded in battle on June 22, 1864, at Kenesaw Mountain in Virginia and his good friend Frank Penniman was killed. Indeed, one third of the company was killed in this battle. Ryder was treated at the field hospital and eventually returned to his regiment.

In April of 1865, church bells rang in Yarmouth. The war was over. But only a few days later they rang again in mourning for the death of President Lincoln. Charles Swift, publisher of *The Register* wrote:

> "Little is talked of but the awful calamity of last week. A heavy gloom rests upon the village, and increases day by

day, as the people begin to realize the melancholy fact that ABRAHAM LINCOLN has been brutally murdered."

On May 24, 1865, John J. Ryder and his fellow soldiers received orders to return home. They arrived in time to celebrate the fourth of July with their friends and families.

The Civil War had a profound effect on Cape Cod. The Cape's maritime economy never returned to the robust trading and fishing activity enjoyed prior to the war. As key industries, shipping and fishing along with the era they represented had ended. In order to find employment, many young men left the Cape. Captains and fishermen sold their ships and became tradesmen or merchants. Some retired. With the lack of a strong economy, the Cape's population declined. Once again, the winds of change were blowing over Cape Cod.

For Sale.

 Schooner HOCKANOM, of Yarmouth, burden 63 82-95ths tons, built at Newburg in the year 1816, well found in sails, rigging, &c., and suitable for cod or mackerel fishing.—
Apply to   JAMES B. CROCKER.
Yarmouth Port, Jan. 6, 1862.   tf

" THREE CHEERS FOR THE RED WHITE AND BLUE."

Ships were sold during the war
Courtesy of *The Register*

Postwar Lifestyle Changes

An era ended with the last third of the 1800s and our nation changed, driven by expansion of manufacturing and transportation. The new century brought with it a turning point in the way people lived on the Cape and new business came to town. Cape Cod had been *discovered* and people came to spend their summers on the Cape's beautiful beaches. In 1900, *The Register* speculated optimistically on the future.

> "... A comparison with the state figures of 1895 shows that a recovery of lost population has set in caused by the summer resort business of the region, which also in some cases leads to permanent residence here. There seems much reason to expect this gain will be maintained and that when the attractions of our shores and inland waters are made known, the County will become not only the resort of those enjoying aquatic sports, but the sanitarium of the whole country."[8]

Tourism was just what the Cape's sagging economy needed and with this expanded business came changes needed by the expanding permanent population. Some changes involved enhanced community services predicated on expanded community cooperation and funding. For example, by 1902, Yarmouth's population had increased so much that the Yarmouth High School graduated 162 students. Such an increase put school expansion high on the town's agenda.

People sold their horses and cows as Yarmouth became a modern, urban community. Roads were built, lamp posts installed and fences removed to make way for automobiles and lawns.

Technological progress changed the way people communicated. No longer was it necessary to travel slowly by foot or horse-drawn carriage to speak with friends or learn of current events. Now one could telephone a business associate over great distances, listen to music or news coming as if by magic from the wireless radio or travel long distances in an automobile at miles per hour rather than miles per day. Instant gratification seemed at hand.

The pace of everyday existence picked up all across Cape Cod. Equally important, the effort needed to ensure survival decreased, allowing people to devote more of their time, energy and funds to what we now call *quality of life* or leisure activities. Citizens' desire that their towns look their best in order to attract tourists and please residents resulted in beautification projects of public streets and buildings. Volunteer improvement societies formed within towns to make sure buildings and streets were attractive and residents of Yarmouth contributed both time and money to this end. In 1911, the Thacher family donated funds to build a one-thousand foot boardwalk across the marsh to the bath houses and beach beyond today's Bass Hole on Cape Cod Bay. At that time, the beach stretched roughly a mile from Mill Creek, east to Bass Hole, a region that now is tidal wetland. Today, a short section of boardwalk remains, allowing one exceptional views of the ever-changing salt marsh.

Social activities filled leisure hours with opportunities for learning and camaraderie. During the late 1800s and early 1900s, citizens formed meeting clubs such as the Owl Club, founded in 1892 in South Yarmouth, which gave dinners and promoted baseball games. The Friday Club, formed by women of the First Congregational Church of Yarmouth in 1901, aided Yarmouth's charitable concerns and remains an active club even today. The Lyceum, built by the Lyceum Hall Company for the promotion of education and learning, kept calendars full with lectures, graduations and social events. Recreational boating became a favorite activity. The Bass River Yacht Club held Saturday catboat races, drawing both participants and spectators.

Social and political changes rapidly came as exemplified by the women's rights movement working for women's suffrage. In August, 1915, hundreds of people supported this cause at a rally held in South Yarmouth at the Owl Club.

But once again, peace had ended. Europe was suffering from World War I, the *Great War, The War that would End All Wars,* the war that would change the political, economic and social structure of nearly all societies, including those of Cape Cod. On July 28, 1914, Austria-Hungary declared war on Russia. From August first through the third, Germany declared war on Russia and France, and on the fourth invaded Belgium. Also on August fourth, Great Britain declared war on Germany. The war that no one wanted was underway. The following year, 1915, the war escalated when on February fourth, Germany declared a submarine blockade of Great Britain, considering any boat approaching England a legitimate military target. Death and destruction became enormous. In July, 1916, an estimated one million casualties occurred during one battle alone, the Battle of the Somme in France, with no significant gains by the western allies.

World War I

In 1916, Cape Cod began to experience the Great War. On October 7, 1916, the *Cape Cod Times* wrote about, Wilma Tucciarone:

"... [Wilma Tucciarone] was just seven years old when she, her grandmother, mother and younger sister and brother had an experience that they would not forget. They had visited relatives in Nova Scotia, and were headed home to Hempstead, New York aboard the Stephano, a British passenger and cargo ship. When the Stephano was 50 miles off Nantucket, it came under attack by a German U-boat." Wilma recalled the incident as follows, "... I'd been on small boats before, but traveling on a boat like the Stephano was a big event for a 7-year old....It was about 6 p.m., time for supper, and I remember going down to the dining room with my grandmother. There was a commotion there and everyone was running up to the deck. I was one of those curious children and wanted to know everything that was going on." The article continues to state that, "Unknown to Wilma at the time, the submarine, the U-53, had already fired torpedoes toward the ship. After one crossed the bow, the ship's captain, Clifford Smith, reportedly radioed the U-boat that 47 Americans were on board. The Germans, after eight minutes, fired another one, but it was wide of the bow-probably intentionally.

My mother, sister and brother were on the hallway stairs when one of the crew told them to get into life jackets and get ready to get into the lifeboats, but he didn't say why....My mother was quite upset about that later, because she didn't know what was going on.

She found me on deck and told us we were going on a little trip. Mother was a calm person and she didn't want us to get excited, but she said later she was very nervous.

She never liked water much and couldn't swim." The lifeboat was rescued by The United States torpedo boat, the *Ericson*."[9]

Once all passengers were rescued, *U-53* sank the *Stephano* with torpedo fire. The article concluded with an ironic ending to this tale.

"... Wilma's father, who had remained in Hempstead while his family journeyed, was panic-stricken when he heard about the sinking. He rushed to New York to board a train for Newport, RI where the survivors had been taken, not knowing if his family was among them. On the way to New York, however, he got a speeding ticket – for going 24 mph – and then, while on the train to Newport, missed his family going the other way."

On April 6, 1917, The United States declared war on Germany. Once again, Cape Cod towns were changed by the call to battle. Many young men volunteered for military service while others were drafted to serve their country. At first, men between the ages of twenty-one and thirty-one were required to register for the draft but as the war intensified the draft age was expanded to include men between eighteen and forty-five.

Posters and advertisements urged people to buy Liberty Bonds, government bonds issued to help fund the war effort. Patriotic women participated by joining the American Red Cross. In Truro, marines organized a *Home Guard* unit open to all men between the ages of 16 and 60. Local papers were filled with poster ads encouraging young men to join the service and young women to join the nursing corps. Those who remained at home were urged to conserve food and to be thrifty. On June 1, 1918, *The Register* wrote:

"The Public Safety Committee and other war emergency committees of Yarmouth are contemplating the starting of a Community Canning Kitchen in the school building where people can bring or send their products to be canned for them at a small cost. The object of this work is to increase the amount of canning done and to eliminate any possible waste of surplus garden or orchard produce. They wish to place the price for canning so that it will merely cover the cost of labor, fuel and incidental expenses."

On July 21, 1918, Orleans became the only location on American soil to receive enemy fire. Mary Heaton Vorse, author of *Time And The Town – A Provincetown Chronicle,* wrote of a German submarine, *U-156*, and its confrontation with the *Perth Amboy*, a steel tug towing a string of barges. For an hour and a half while in full view of land, the German submarine fired 147 rounds without interference from the U.S. military. Finally, long after they had abandoned ship, aid came to the *Perth Amboy's* crew from the coastguard station at Chatham. The official account was written by Joseph Perry of Provincetown, captain of the last barge.

"We were just abreast Coast Guard Station No. 40 at Orleans when the German submarine appeared out of the haze one half mile away, firing at us with both guns. She attacked the tug first, and then the four barges, beginning with the stone-laden Lansford, and ending with my vessel, the No. 740. The shells fired at the tug struck with deadly accuracy, but the deep-laden stone barge was hard to hit, most of the shells flying high overhead straight for the beach. We received in turn a hail of shot. Shells struck my craft in the bow. Each one just seemed to lift the deck clear. All hands lost but little time getting away from the vicinity in our boats. I saw two flying machines flying high over the submarine. After a while they straightened out and sped toward Chatham. They returned later in the afternoon after the submarine had disappeared."[10]

The coastguard lookout notified the station off Chatham and the naval station ten miles away. An account by Captain Robert F. Pierce of the station at Chatham stated:

"When about two-thirds of the way off to the sinking tug and four barges we met the boat from the Perth Amboy with all of her crew which had escaped. The crews of the barges had left and were pulling for Nauset Harbor in their lifeboats. They landed three miles from our station to the north. On meeting the lifeboat from the burning tug, Captain Tapley of the Perth Amboy said: 'Do not go any further; we have all our crew here and all have left the barges.' No. 1 surfman, W. D. Moore, was put into the lifeboat of the Perth Amboy at the request of Captain Tapley to treat the injured man and to render first aid to the seaman who had been so badly injured in the pilot house. He was lying in the stern of the boat with a badly shattered arm and unconscious from the loss of blood. Mr. Moore at once put a tourniquet on the arm to stop the flow of blood from an arterial hemorrhage and treated the wound of another man who was near him, and assisted in landing the lifeboat through the surf. After landing, the services of a doctor were obtained and the crew of the Perth Amboy were removed to the station. The doctor treated the remaining injured men, and complimented Mr. Moore, surfman No. 1, on his work with the tourniquet, saying: 'Whoever put this tourniquet on this man saved him from bleeding to death.'"[11]

Spectators rushed to the scene from as far away as Provincetown to see the action first hand and hundreds lined the shore to see enemy submarine *U-156*. A captain by the name of Kendrick stood by his boat offering one dollar round trip tours to see the submarine close at hand. He stated, however, that he could not promise anything. When asked if he meant that he could not promise safe accommodations, Kendrick replied, *Safety, shucks no! I* won't promise that the submarine won't 'a' submerged, and you won't waste your dollar. Those who paid the fee were disappointed as the submarine submerged and departed before they arrived.

A Cape Cod WW I Vet's Story

Basil Dandison, *Bumps* to his son *Bo*, was a 102 year old Cape Cod resident who served his country during the Great War. In 2002, *Bumps* told of his experiences with a vivid memory. As a high school sophomore in Michigan, he enlisted to serve his country, looking forward with enthusiasm to trench warfare in France. When he and his comrades learned that they were headed for Marine training at Parris Island rather than the French trenches, they were all disappointed.

Bumps knew how to manage a store, having learned the grocery business from his father, and the Marines took full advantage of this skill. Parris Island was short of chief stewards and so *Bumps* was asked to manage the Post Exchange, commonly known as the PX. But managing a store was not what he had in mind for his military career.

Feeling that he *wasn't going anywhere* as a store manager, *Bumps* found service on the USS Maryland, a newly commissioned navel vessel. He served for eighteen months aboard the Maryland, assigned as Corporal of the guard. When asked his combat position he replied, *I was called captain of the five inch gun.* This gun fired a sixty pound projectile a distance of eight miles. He opened the gun's breech to permit shell and powder loading and then closed the breech. Once the five inch gun was loaded, he called out the shot being fired.

After completing military service with an honorable discharge in 1923, *Bumps* returned home to finish high school. The fact he was now twenty-three, quite a bit older than his classmates, did not deter him. He continued his education and graduated from the University of Michigan in 1929. In 1939, he joined the publishing firm of McGraw-Hill and worked his way up to the position of executive vice president of McGraw-Hill International Corporation. As senior vice president, he launched publishing programs in Europe and Asia, including International Student Editions which sold low-cost reprints of texts to students overseas. In this capacity he visited seventy countries and was honored as one of the first persons to circumnavigate the world in a commercial airline. He received the Export Award from President John F. Kennedy, which honored McGraw-Hill as the only U.S. publisher to successfully distribute textbooks overseas.

Basil Dandison and his son were U.S. Marines
Photo by the author

When *Bumps* retired he did not stop working. He continued as a consultant to publishers and engaged in overseas assignments for the U.S. Agency for

International Development and the International Executive Service Corps where he worked until the age of 90.

When asked what would make the world a better place today, *Bumps* replied, *We must think about the needs of life and do the best we can. We must not take things for granted. We need to be more vigilant.*[12]

Wartime significantly reduced Cape tourism and the economy lost momentum. Local businessmen pursued new interests hoping to create year-round work. In 1916, the Bay State Freezer Company built a five story building to house their sixty-five ton refrigeration unit which allowed them to freeze two to three hundred barrels of fish each day. Yarmouth had high expectations that The Bay State Freezer Company would provide a strong and lasting economic boost to the town. Indeed, men from Yarmouth and those of surrounding towns were employed at the company. Unfortunately, reality and expectations do not always meet and the Bay State Freezer Company closed it's doors in 1922.

Economic Ups And Downs

After World War I, tourism increased and Cape Cod's real estate business took off. In 1926, there were so many real estate transactions that Yarmouth's Registrar of Deeds could not keep up with the paperwork. Real estate activity grew steadily all across Cape Cod fueling growth of other businesses, including banking. The Cape Cod Cooperative Bank was established during this time.

People traveled more than ever as automobiles became common. Indeed, automobiles catalyzed economic growth throughout the country, changing the way people lived their lives and perceived distance. Popular acceptance of automobiles was astounding. In 1929, the United States produced eighty-five percent of the automobiles manufactured world-wide.

Food packaging and processing companies such as Heinz, Borden and Campbell thrived, as did the American Tobacco Company. Employment was high, especially in the chemical and electrical industries. Engineers, physicists and chemists were recruited to invent and improve products by companies such as DuPont, General Electric, Allied Chemical and Eastman Kodak.

Economic disruption that began in October, 1929, with the stock market collapse, began to abate as the 1930s ended. But in spite of the depression, the Cape's character was altered forever during the 1930s as people moved from their farms into rapidly growing towns and as they replaced shoreline summer cottages with year-round homes. Between 1930 and 1940, Yarmouth's population grew 27 percent and the number of houses increased 57 percent.[13] New job opportunities were created as agricultural Yarmouth became a rapidly expanding business community. All of Cape Cod enjoyed a similar transformation.

To accommodate the needs of a growing town, Yarmouth's government was forced to grow as well. Assistant assessors and registrars were hired as was an assistant police chief. Residents still enjoyed animals but rather than raising farm animals, they acquired dogs as pets The town was forced to hire a pet control officer as the number of dog licenses increased from 169 to 213. By

1931, town government had grown so much that town offices had to remain open five days a week. People of Yarmouth and all of Cape Cod had found a new way of life.

In 1936, Yarmouth's planning board called a meeting to discuss protection of historical landmarks. Two items on the agenda were removal of roadside billboards and planning, consistent with maintaining the Cape's natural beauty. A letter read at this meeting written by Joseph C. Lincoln states:

"The preserving of Cape Cod, as Cape Cod is, in my opinion a vitally important subject for consideration by Cape people. We are adding to our summer population each year. The great majority of visitors to our country have been attracted to it because of its individuality, its simplicity, the charm which is its own. There are thousands of seaside resorts, but only one Cape Cod.

I am convinced [people] should do everything in their power to save the old buildings and landmarks, to keep our picturesque roads and streets from becoming city boulevards, to preserve the genuine Cape Cod flavor, where it is possible.

Whenever a movement is on foot to save and preserve the real Cape Cod it should have the support of us all."[14]

At a national level, the expansion and enthusiasm characteristic of the 1920s were dashed by the economic events of the 1930s as the country suffered from *The Great Depression*. Jobs which had been plentiful only a few years earlier became scarce as businesses closed. On Cape Cod, the depression slowed the economy during the early years but as the Cape was still primarily an agricultural society, the impact was not as severe as it was in other parts of the country.

Meanwhile, as issues of town expansion, beautification, regional planning and economic boom and bust brewed on Cape Cod and much of the country, Europe and Asia embarked on yet another devastating major conflict. At first most Americans believed that World War II would not impact the United States but on Cape Cod this perspective changed as people recognized that the Cape extends far into the Atlantic Ocean and as the military began constructing Camp Edwards.

World War II

Camp Edwards

Camp Edwards was named for Major General Clarence R. Edwards, Commander of the Yankee Division in France during 1917-1918. Captain Fred E. Brake described the camp's environment:

> "... It is an area of 19 square miles in the South-West part of Cape Cod, about 10 miles from the mouth of the Cape Cod Canal and in the Townships of Falmouth, Sandwich and Bourne. The Camp proper is in the South-East corner of the Reservation. It is on a small level plain that in the past has had little value except as a sheep pasture. Around it is rough terrain covered with a scrub pine forest. This type of country is excellent for maneuvers, training, map making, etc. The 30 square mile Shawme State Forest, not part of the Reservation, forms an excellent buffer for artillery practice."[15]

The sheep pasture was *The Coonamessett Ranch* and its transformation was reported by *The Register.*

"In April 1935, Massachusetts Gov. James Michael Curley took pen to paper on Beacon Hill and signed into law a bill to use $100,000 of the state's money to buy a huge tract of land on Cape Cod. The purpose? To give the National Guard and other military branches a place to train.

By the end of the year, the state's military hierarchy had come into possession of 34 square miles of Cape Cod, almost one-tenth of the entire peninsula. Land that several years earlier speculators had bought and called *The Coonamessett Ranch*, the self-styled 'largest sheep ranch east of the Mississippi' became the Massachusetts Military Reservation."[16]

Camp Edwards was a city in its own right, eventually including facilities for housing, hospitalization, recreation and entertainment required by a population of approximately 30,000 soldiers. Construction speed was paramount and efficiency was the first priority of the camp's builders and engineers. Planning and scheduling were critical. For example, building foundations had to be installed on a schedule that allowed a peak crew of 10,000 carpenters to construct buildings. Plumbers, electricians and sheet metal workers all had to merge their efforts with those of carpenters and one another. At its peak, the project involved approximately 18,000 workers. Construction delays were simply not an option.

Railroad track to Camp Edwards was laid from Woods Hole, joining the Buzzards Bay branch of the New York, New Haven and Hartford Railroad. Camp Edwards was equipped with full railroad facilities including an embarkation area, a coal storage yard, five spurs running beside the Quartermaster Depot Warehouses and a short line leading to the Cold Storage building. The Cold

Storage building was the camp's only reinforced concrete building and it was to this cork lined building that perishable foods, carried in refrigerated cars, were transported. Concrete was also used in the camp's sewage treatment plant, one of the most modern plants of the time.

Camp Edwards, October 10, 1940
Photo courtesy of *The Register*

Camp Edwards' hospital consisted of eighty buildings connected to one another by enclosed runways. In addition to receiving patients from Army units, the hospital met the needs of all Cape and Island military installations. By 1945, it had 3,200 beds. Camp Edwards was also home to two additional hospitals intended to meet special needs. The Debarkation Hospital, built in July, 1944, accepted sick and wounded men from Europe. Here, wounded soldiers received initial treatment and were prepared for transfer to permanent hospitalization, hopefully near their homes. Approximately 30,000 patients passed through this hospital. The Convalescent Hospital, built in February, 1945, with a capacity of 6,000, received only ambulatory patients. After treatment at this facility, men were usually discharged. Ambulatory patients lived in two story barracks remodeled to house fifty-one patients rather than the usual sixty-three. The facility included a large swimming pool for recreation and therapy. Approximately 10,000 patients passed through this facility.

Brake's description of Camp Edwards tells of its enormity:

> "... The majority of the buildings of the Camp are arranged around a parade ground three quarters of a mile square, the sides of which are roughly along the points of the compass. Each side is known as a zone. Thus there are the North, East, South and West zone. Each zone is broken up into regimental areas of which there are four in the North, three in the East, three in the South and three in the West; thirteen in all. Two roads parallel to each other run around the parade ground. Each regimental area is built like the next. Cottages for Brigade and regimental Commanding Officers, Officers' Quarters and Mess, and Regimental Administration buildings, namely: a half dozen double company supply houses, a Post Exchange, an Infirmary, a Recreation Hall, equipped with a projection room for moving pictures and a stage for formal and informal theatrical entertainment, a Guard House, a dozen to fifteen Day Rooms, where the soldiers may read and play games, and the same number of Mess Halls. Across the Outer Road are the rows and rows of Barracks, each capable of housing 63 men. There are a total of 471 of them in the Camp. ... Beyond the Barracks are the Motor Repair Shops, Gasoline Stations and Truck Parks; all the facilities inherent to the mechanization and motorization of our modern Army."[17]

Camp Edwards was constructed of 50 million board feet of lumber. With all this wood, fire was a major concern and so each regimental area was separated by a 250 foot wide fire-break. Fire stations were built in positions that allowed all buildings to be within three-eighths of a mile of fire equipment. Sixty trained firemen were assigned to Camp Edwards and a full alert was maintained around the clock.

Logistics to deal with 18,000 workmen were complex, to say the least. Some workers commuted daily from Lawrence and Lowell, a hundred miles away. One can easily imagine horrendous traffic problems. Sometimes traffic back-ups extended fifteen miles from the Camp. During peak construction, payroll ran to one million dollars each week. In order to maintain work and still allow workers to collect their wages, an armored paymaster's caravan of trucks and busses went from station to station within the camp.

As construction of Camp Edwards reached completion, soldiers arrived for training and workmen were laid off, hundreds being dropped daily from the payroll. One week there were 12,000 workmen and 2,000 soldiers at the Camp. The next week there were 2,000 workmen and 12,000 soldiers.

As a consequence of the tremendous increase in local population, Camp Edwards had a major impact on its neighbor, Falmouth. Not only were there thousands of soldiers on the base, but also there were soldiers' families and visitors in need of accommodations. Young brides looking for their husbands made their way to Cape Cod only to run short of funds and become lost. Life was different in this New England tourist area from that in their rural home towns and they did not have enough money for housing. United Service Organization staff workers were overwhelmed as young women arrived on the Cape with no idea how to reach their husbands. With high Cape Cod prices, the women needed employment in order to stay. Rent was expensive with rates rising by the week. Within three months, the price of lodging doubled. Both the town and the new brides were bewildered by the rapidly changing circumstances.

After the war, Camp Edwards became inactive in June, 1946, but was re-opened on August 9, 1950, to support the Korean War. The *Cape Cod Times* reported:

> "*Citizen-Soldiers* from all over the country again came to Cape Cod, and the tempo of building, training and planning increased to a level similar to that of the 40s.
>
> In late 1954, Congress authorized the transfer of Camp Edwards from the Department of the Army to the Department of the Air Force for the purpose of operating a military airfield with supporting facilities."

Because Camp Edwards was a secure military facility on the eastern edge of the country, the Air Force housed nuclear BOMARC missiles on the base, each in its own building. BOMARC is an acronym for <u>Bo</u>eing <u>M</u>ichigan <u>A</u>eronautical <u>R</u>esearch <u>C</u>enter. There were reportedly 56 of these nuclear weapons stored in a secure, off-limits compound on the base. According to *The Register:*

> "The BOMARC was meant to be the last line of defense against a Russian nuclear attack. The idea was that if Russian planes got close to shore, the BOMARCs would be fired. The atomic bombs on the BOMARCs would explode over us, obliterating the attacking planes with their own nuclear payloads. Presumably, the fallout and devastation caused by our own bombs would be less than what the Russians would have dropped.
>
> ... The BOMARCs were never fired, of course. Even if the dubious theory they operated under was plausible, they became obsolete almost immediately; intercontinental ballistic missiles rendered them superfluous.

While people at the time took great care in handling the bombs and radioactive material associated with the BOMARCs, their secret, closed facility took much poorer care of the fuels and fuels that were needed to keep the missiles poised. The BOMARC site became one of the most serious environmental catastrophes on Cape Cod, polluting millions of gallons of water as chemicals from it seeped south and into the aquifer."[18]

A BOMARC Missile
Photo by Barry Donahue; Photo courtesy of *The Register.*

Today, Camp Edwards is once again a center of attention, but for a very different reason. No longer are building and training exciting activities. There are toxic contaminants in the ground water beneath Camp Edwards, part of the Cape's fresh water aquifer.

Military exercises, including firing of artillery and mortar ordinance, left significant quantities of contaminates on the ground and these, along with contamination from the BOMARC missile site, seeped into the aquifer. Indeed, contamination is far more extensive than anyone expected. One hundred test wells dug in and around the artillery impact area showed sufficient groundwater contamination to cause great public concern and prompted the Army immediately to initiate cleanup procedures. In an article written by Kevin Dennehy, The *Cape Cod Times* described the extent of contamination:

> "... Perchlorate is among the toxic chemicals found in the water and beyond the base fence line. When it was found in Bourne Water District wells, district officials shut down three of the six wells that supply water to more than 10,000 people.
>
> Cleanup will begin in an old explosives dumping area called Demolition Area 1."

Dennehy wrote of a 7,000-foot plume of explosive components and perchlorate which now edges toward Bourne.

> "... The contamination plume is at least 3,000 to 3,500 feet from the Bourne border – traveling about a foot or two a day. Perchlorate, a compound of rocket propellant, has been found in high concentrations near Demolition Area 1 and along the Sandwich border, where defense contractors had conducted weapons tests."[o]
>
> "The Army Guard has three approaches for cleanup in Demolition Area 1. They include:
>
> Installing one or two wells to remove tainted water at the leading edge of the plume, to stem the plume's progress toward Bourne.
>
> Plant a series of wells in the heart of the plume, to remove the highest concentrations of chemicals.

---

[o] Perchlorate is a negatively charged ion associated with a positively charged ion to form a neutral salt. Perchlorate is a strong oxidizing agent and a common ingredient of explosive materials.

Install a series of wells along the plume's spine to suck the toxic chemicals toward the plume's center, so that it narrows and eventually collapses."[19]

Environmental Protection Agency officials were surprised at the extent of contamination found. In fact, contamination plumes were moving off base. Of one hundred monitoring wells drilled at Camp Edwards, fifty three showed contamination exceeding health standards. A report sited by EPA officials predicted a drinking water shortfall of 9.8 to 11 million gallons a day among Upper Cape towns by 2020 as a consequence of contamination from Camp Edwards. Needless to say, this remains a serious concern for Cape residents and state officials alike.

The Oceanographic Institution

The Woods Hole Oceanographic Institution, WHOI, played an interesting role in World War II as described by The *Falmouth Enterprise*:

"Soldiers who went ashore through surf in North Africa, Sicily, Normandy and various Pacific islands had, as one of their protections, painstaking hours of research and prediction which gave their commanders foreknowledge of wave conditions on the beaches. ... Oceanographic Institution at Woods Hole was the source of some of the vital information upon which commanders of amphibious assaults based their schedules for invasions."[20]

Questions that needed answers in support of successful landing operations included how strong the tide would be, how high the waves would be, how strong the surf would be and how deep or shallow the water would be. Answers to these questions were needed in order to specify landing craft sizes and the techniques that would be used in landing. In order to optimize chances for successful landings, times of the most favorable surf conditions at specific landing sites were needed. Early in the war, when amphibious landings were being discussed, the Navy turned to the Oceanographic Institution for answers. Prior to this, no one had attempted prediction of wave characteristics from storm data.

One factor that does not change as a wave rushes toward shore is the time between it and the next wave. This interval is nearly constant from the wave's origin until the wave approaches the shoreline, a distance which can exceed 500 miles. The height and length of the wave may change but not the time between it and the next wave.

After arrangements were made with Coast Guard officials, WHOI investigators established observation stations along the coast at South Beach, Martha's Vineyard, New Jersey, North Carolina, Highland Light and Plum Island near the Ipswich River. Observers monitored the surf and from information gained, investigators were first able to characterize patterns of wave behavior and then develop predictive tools for average surf conditions. Using these newly developed predictive models in conjunction with conditions reported at sea, scientists were able to predict shore conditions. By reverse reasoning, observers' knowledge of shore conditions resulted in knowledge of sea conditions. Eventually, human observers of wave characteristics were replaced by recording instruments.

Work undertaken at Woods Hole impacted the course of the war. In 1943, a storm made it impossible for General Patton's Seventh Army to land on Sicily. Both German and Italian armies expected the surf to run high for some time after the storm subsided as this was the usual course following a storm with high winds. However, surf forecasting based on Woods Hole work correctly predicted that the surf would quickly subside. Armed with this information, the invasion fleet moved in and took the enemy by surprise.

Surf forecasting also helped pilots. Using the prediction formulae, bomber pilots estimated a ship's speed from the wave pattern of its wake. Seaplane pilots learned that the best landings in heavy seas could be made cross-wind, parallel to wave crests and in the trough between them.

Childhood War Effort

Patriotism was strong during World War II and children of Cape Cod helped the war effort. Anne N. Harmon wrote of her WW II memories in her book *Ambergris and Arrowheads: Growing up on Cape Cod In the 1930s and 1940s*. Ann, who grew up in Osterville, described how she and her friends helped the war effort:

> "... The day after Pearl Harbor, our elementary school principal, Lida Sherman, gave us a long talk. We all felt the shock and thrill of being at war, although we had no real conception of what it really meant. Miss Sherman tried to impress upon us how things would change in our lives. She said that we must be brave and patriotic and as a school we must work together to help any way we could."[21]

An airplane spotting program was put in place soon after the attack on Pearl Harbor. On the roof of the town community center stood a small spotter's tower that one reached by climbing stairs on the side of the building. Inside was a room with windows on all sides. A chart on one wall showed silhouettes of different kinds of German and U.S. aircraft.

School children, accompanied by an adult, helped cover the observation shifts in the tower and logged each plane they spotted overhead. Each child who helped with this endeavor was given a certificate for time they served in the tower.

Children also participated in the *fat parade.* After collecting leftover grease from their mother's weekly cooking, children joined their classmates and along with their teacher, Miss Sherman, marched to the First National store. At the store, the containers of grease were weighed, emptied into a common container and given back to the children to be refilled during the next week.

This project was thoroughly enjoyed by school children as they were allowed to leave school to march to the store while at the same time they understood that they were doing something important to help win the war. Money the school received for the grease was used to send *Reader's Digest* subscriptions to active servicemen from the village. The fat itself was used to make soap.

Children were excused from school to gather milkweed pods which they were told not to open as doing so caused the seeds to disperse. The silk in the milkweed pods was used to fill life jackets. Children also collected scrap metal which was placed in a large pile in the center of the village from where it was recycled into war material. They even recycled empty toothpaste tubes, which at that time were made of lead.

Because so many men were in the service, girls and boys were able to leave traditional roles and do jobs that were not ordinarily open to them. They mowed lawns, delivered groceries and even caddied on golf courses. These were new experiences for children, especially girls, and they relished the experience of stepping out of tradition.

Harmon described the town's excitement when the war finally ended.

> "... When the war ended with Germany, we rang the bells in the churches and when Japan finally surrendered, I went to the church to help my grandfather ring the bells again. The sirens wailed, horns tooted and people came into the church to give thanks. Some people started singing *God Bless America.*"[22]

Ceremonies were held, speeches given and a monument built in Osterville's center. Years later, Harmon returned to the monument to read the names. One hundred fifty-three from Osterville had served in the armed forces, five of whom had not returned. Harmon reflected, *I thought back to those war days. We were only children, but we had tried to do our part to help the war effort.*

The Men Who Served

Children did their part for the war effort as did the men who joined the service. On Friday, December 7, 2001, the 60th anniversary of the attack on Pearl Harbor, World War II veterans told their wartime experiences to students of Chatham High School. The *Cape Cod Times* reported the stories of soldiers who survived the surprise Japanese attack and those who participated in the D-Day assault on Europe's beaches:

> "... Daylight was barely an hour old when Walter Morley heard the alarm on the morning of Dec. 7, 1941.
>
> He scrambled onto the deck of the USS Bagley just in time to see a Japanese torpedo plane skimming the surface of the water. Seconds later, the stern of the

battleship USS West Virginia exploded. 'I can still see the sun glinting off the wing.'

... From the deck of the USS Whitney, George Bannan could see the Japanese planes bomb other ships in the harbor, causing men to pour out of every opening. 'It was like kicking an anthill with your feet,' he said."

On June 6, 1944, D-Day, an armada comprised of 5,000 ships, boats and amphibious craft carried a quarter of a million soldiers from the United States, Britain and Canada across the English Channel to begin the direct assault on German occupied France. At the end of the day the Allies were in command of a large coastal area.

A retired postal worker from Sandwich, Pfc. John MacPhee told his story to Trevor Maxwell, a staff writer for the *Cape Cod Times*. In the article "Everyone has a story to tell", Maxwell reported that, "Pfc. John MacPhee fell into the choppy water with 36 pounds of dynamite on his back, three food rations, an M-1 rifle and a single terrifying thought: 'I'll never make that beach.'

He saw bursts of gunfire through the fog and bodies of soldiers in his company pulled under the waves. Behind them, 16-inch guns boomed from the deck of the USS Texas. June 6, 1944. 6:30 a.m.

... He struggled for footing at Omaha Beach, weighed down by a soaked uniform and nearly 100 pounds of gear. Just as MacPhee began his rush up the sand, he was struck by shrapnel. Then bullets hit both of his legs and shattered the humorous bone in his left arm."[23]

Only 20 years old, MacPhee's chances of surviving such conditions were slim but he was saved by two other soldiers and lived to share his story with fifteen other survivors when he was seventy-eight years old. At a dinner with Cape Cod veterans, wives and widows of D-

Day, MacPhee was one of many who shared their experiences.

After being wounded at Omaha Beach, MacPhee was treated in a makeshift hospital in Normandy and eventually transferred to a hospital in Massachusetts. He now has limited motion in his left arm and there are still three bullets lodged in his body.

Economy Effected By The War

From 1941 to 1960 there was incredible growth on Cape Cod. The population of Yarmouth doubled and property values climbed. With such rapid expansion, zoning laws were considered to control the nature and location of building and commercial growth, and in 1946 a zoning law was approved by 90% of the vote at the annual town meeting.

World War II brought an end to the depression and once again Cape Codders responded to changes presented to them. A few years before the war, Charles J. Fish identified a previously unknown variety of clam, the black quahog, a large version of the prolific hard clam. Fish, who worked at the Narragansett Marine Laboratory, recognized this clam as a new food source. It wasn't long before a government contract was negotiated to furnish black quahogs to Camp Edwards and other Army training centers. After the war, black quahogs went public as mahogany clams, a more attractive name chosen to enhance sales. Lobster, crab, oyster and scallop fishermen were also doing well.

Narragansett Bay and the waters surrounding Cape Cod share many characteristics and industries including aspects of commercial and recreational boating as well as fishing and shell fishing.

The war had brought major shipping to Narragansett Bay which was a base for naval and cargo ships. Freighters arrived empty and departed with supplies. Shipbuilding began at the Rheem Shipyard in Providence, RI, employing several thousand civilian workers. PT boats were tested at fifty miles per hour across parts of upper Narragansett Bay. More than ten thousand soldiers were stationed in the forts at the mouth of the Bay and soldiers were also stationed in beach-front cottages.

With the end of the war, economic improvements came to both the Narragansett Bay and Cape Cod regions as a peacetime economy re-emerged and many of the developments in these areas paralleled one another.

Recreational boating returned as a leisure-time activity, reviving the small-boat building industry. Initially, wooden boats, some constructed of plywood, dominated the industry but these were difficult for owners to maintain. Then fiberglass appeared, ushering in new boat construction methods and boats that were relatively easy and inexpensive to maintain. Fiberglas changed the boating industry. Soon, Cape Cod Bay on the north side and Nantucket Sound on the south were filled with both power and sail boats constructed with fiberglass hulls.

Boating has never been an inexpensive recreation. However, post-war prosperity, shorter working hours and longer vacations made it possible for more people to enjoy water sports. Marine industries increased to such an extent that they soon became the third most important factor in the Narragansett Bay economy, behind the U.S. Navy and commercial shipping. Recreational boat builders, marinas, marine supply houses, dealers of new and used boats, and, of course, bait and tackle shops flourished there and on Cape Cod.

Improvements in outboard motors had as much impact on recreational boating as did fiberglass. Although they were not new to the boating world, outboard motors became bigger, sturdier, more powerful and much more dependable.

Even the quahog industry was effected by large outboard motors. Flat-bottomed boats outfitted with large motors allowed Narragansett Bay fishermen to travel at thirty to forty miles an hour. Being able to travel at this speed allowed fishermen to outrun conservation officers who were trying to stop them from working in polluted waters or from taking undersized quahogs. Finally, with the development of the Boston Whaler, the harbor patrol could, with a 100-horsepower outboard motor, lifejackets and crash helmets, achieve the fifty miles an hour needed to catch wayward fishermen.

Local newspapers excitedly reported motor boat chases that occurred during what was known as the *Narragansett Bay quahog wars.* One news report told of illegal nightly quahog harvesting in polluted Greenwich Cove that produced one of the larger crops of *little necks* in Rhode Island. Along with undersized clams, polluted clams were bagged and transported to areas such as Scranton, PA, where they sold in competition with legal shellfish harvested from Narragansett Bay.

Concern of conservation officials was justified as pollution became a serious matter. Commercial contracts generated as much as $2,500,000 a year for the benefit of fishermen and processors. If disease outside of Rhode Island were traced to Narragansett Bay shellfish, the

Public Health Service would be able to cancel interstate shellfish shipping. This threat had a significant impact on the Health Service's ability to enforce rules. On site, conservation officers were able to enforce shellfishing rules by using faster boats and two-way radios which facilitated coordination of land and water forces. Also, it was helpful that district court judges began taking stern stands on shellfish violations and enforced rules regarding fishing in polluted waters. Once the *quahog wars* ended and conservation rules were enforced in the mid-1950s, fishermen turned to smaller, less expensive motors.

Tanker traffic was a leading commercial operation on Narragansett Bay after World War II. Tankers arrived at the head of the Bay with petroleum for tank farms in Providence and East Providence or for pipeline transmission to Massachusetts. In support of this traffic, the channel was dredged to forty feet and dredging of rocky areas in the upper Bay was accomplished in 1977. The Navy remained Narragansett Bay's strongest economic force and was Rhode Island's largest civilian employer during the twenty-five years following World War II.

A Bridge Across Time
This is a story of two people. One, a World War II soldier, the other a nephew of that soldier. The story of these two people expresses the heart of the war. War impacts not only soldiers who fight them, but also people born after the battles are fought. As one reads the story of these two men, one senses that a bridge has stretched across time in order to bring a family together.

The *Cape Cod Times* wrote the amazing six part story about one soldier's return home from World War II. Bob Sanders did not make it home alive, and it was not until sixty years later that his nephew, Rob Sanders, born fifteen years after his uncle's last mission, began a remarkable search to find where his uncle was buried. Bob Sanders had written his mother that *It doesn't matter whether I'm dead or alive, I just want to come home.* Rob's mission was to carry out his uncle's request and bring him home to Brewster, Massachusetts.

Bob Sanders was an Army Air Corps gunner at age twenty-two. On August 22, 1944, his B-24 bomber went down over Vienna, Austria. His mother, Ruth, could not accept Bob's death and in her denial would not give the Army instructions as to what to do with her son's body. She refused to answer letters sent by the army or answer the door when officials came to speak directly with her. Consequently, Bob Sanders was buried and reburied across Europe in a series of military graves. When Bob's three siblings asked about him, their mother only responded, *That chapter is closed.* The chapter stayed closed until Rob Sanders began his eighteen month search across two continents and four states to fulfill his uncle's wish.

Robin Lord of the Cape Cod Times wrote:

> "In the process, Rob Sanders – a 41-year old Harwich firefighter-paramedic, Air Force reservist, husband and stepfather – became part of a story about how one man's spirit can reach beyond the grave and touch the heart of another.
>
> Rob well knew all about the family taboo. He knew no one was supposed to speculate about where his Uncle Bob might be buried. He knew that, even after his grieving grandmother's death in 1993, the family continued to obey her orders not to talk about her oldest son's death."[24]

Three letters telling of Bob Sanders death came to the large house on Route 6A in Brewster and each time no one responded to them. Because there was no response to the questions of what to do with the body, Bob was buried without a funeral. Although War Department officials continued to send letters and went to the house, Ruth Sanders continued to avoid the fact of her son's death.

Bob Sanders, Ruth's oldest son, was good looking, a star baseball player, smart and considerate. A childhood friend who lived across the street remembered Bob … *trying to help his struggling mother. Ruth Sanders was raising four children without their father, who had left when Bob was a young boy. The family did what it could to get by. To keep out the winter cold, they banked the house's foundation with sea grass and burned wood for fuel.* Bob and his friend Ted Ellis picked beach plums or blueberries and caddied at the Brewster Golf Course to make extra money.

After graduating from high school, Bob worked at Nickerson State Park as a ranger. When he was 20 he went to Boston and enlisted in the Army. He was chosen for the Army Elite Corps and eventually served as a gunner in Italy with the 15th Air Force. By 1944, at 22 years old, he was a staff sergeant with 49 missions completed. After completing just one more mission, he would have been able to return home. Having served for two years, Bob wanted to go home to Brewster to be with family and friends. For his 50th mission, his plane, a B-24 Liberator, was assigned a bombing run over Vienna.

Describing the Vienna mission, Lord wrote:

> "… Instead, on a stifling hot August day, the plane, in flames, would plummet earthward after receiving its fatal blows. In the chaos, six crew members would parachute into waiting German hands – one of them would die of his wounds in an Austrian hospital, the rest would be released to the Allies after nine months as prisoners of war. Four men, including Bob, would never make it out of the plane."

Fifteen years later, Bob's brother Kent named his only son after his beloved brother. Rob, who looked much like his uncle Bob, joined the Air Force Reserves in 1984. His specialty was search and rescue and he served as a flight medic until 1992 when he became a firefighter. The story of his uncle haunted Rob and he dreamed of one day returning his uncle to home soil. He felt very connected to his look-a-like uncle and in the summer of 1999, when his father gave him a picture of Bob in his flight uniform and told him what information he had of him, Rob began his search. On November 30, 1999, after months of making phone calls and searching the internet, his phone rang.

A Veterans Affairs agent in Providence, Rhode Island, suggested he contact the American Battle Monument Commission. On a Friday afternoon, at 3:45 p.m., Rob Sanders made the call and was told that his uncle was buried in row 37, plot B, grave 7 in the Ardennes Cemetery in Neupre, Belgium. Rob called his wife, Sharon, who worked at Cape Cod Hospital, and with tears streaming down his face simply stated, *I found him.* But for Rob Sanders, this was only part of unraveling a long, lost story.

Bob Sanders' story began to take shape when Rob's father, Kent, found a trunk in the attic of his sister's house. Bob's mother had stored all the memories of her son in this sealed trunk. When at long last the trunk was opened, memories poured out. Inside was a box that had not been opened. It contained an American flag with a note stating that the flag had been used to cover Bob's coffin before interment in the Ardennes Cemetery. There were also blank War Department forms from the late 1940s repeatedly asking what Ruth Sanders wanted done with her son's body. Finally, the trunk held 102 letters Bob had written from November 1942 to August 1944. The last letter had been written only nine days before his death.

> "... His writing spoke of the rigors of gunnery school training, in which he was required to take a machine gun apart and put it back together with a blindfold over his eyes. Money, girlfriends, a drink now and then, and other subjects characteristic of a 22 year-old American man are sprinkled throughout. Mention of war was brief and with the generality required by military censorship.
>
> But the central theme marching through the 22-month parade of letters is family, Cape Cod – and getting back to his Brewster home.
>
> The letters reassured his family that he would safely return home after completing his tour of duty. "The fellow you read about in the paper was killed in a crash. It was just carelessness and those things are bound to happen. Don't worry, because it isn't going to happen to me."[25]

When Bob was in Italy, he wrote of missing the ice cream stand in Brewster and having to miss his sister's birthday party the next year. ... *It's a beautiful day here today and it makes me think a lot of home and the Cape. As you know, the twelfth of June will be my 22nd birthday and I surely hope that I observe the twenty-third back home for good once more.* On June 19, 1944, Bob wrote his mother, ... *It's a little premature to talk about it, but I think if the breaks go my way, I may get home this fall. Boy, it will seem like heaven.*

With each new piece of information, Rob Sanders and his wife Sharon became more determined to put together the pieces of the puzzle of Bob's life. They spent hours on the computer looking at sites on the world wide web that they thought might lead them to information. They had a stroke of luck when they met a man named Norm Dickason through the 15th Air Force Heavy Bombers Association web site. Norm led them to a list of crew members that had served with Bob Sanders. Norm also connected them with a man who finds missing airmen reports for families. Two months later, a forty page report of the mission in which Bob Sanders was killed was in Rob's hands.

The report listed the ten crew members who had been on the B-24's fatal mission. This was not the plane Bob usually flew in and the crew was a pieced-together crew. Bob's usual position was tail gunner. On this mission, however, he was assigned the left waist gunner position. If he had been in his usual position as tail gunner, he probably would have survived the crash.

The pilot, Richard Wellbrock, captured by the Germans after the crash, was able to hide his mission diary in the dirt floor of his prison cell. Wellbrock wrote of flak, shrapnel-loaded mini-bombs preset to explode at specific altitudes, fired by German anti-aircraft guns:

"... We were called for a mission at 3 a.m. and when we arrived at the briefing tent found that our target for the day was Vienna. I had been in the squadron long enough to feel my stomach tightening up at the name Vienna, for other than Ploesti (Romania) and Berlin, it is the worst in Europe today due to the flak gun and fighter plane concentrations that are kept there for protection.

We took off about 5:30 that morning and after assembling were on our way about 7:00.

Just as we went in over Vienna our ship was hit between No. 3 and 4 engines and set on fire. We were knocked into a spin and immediately knew that we were finished, so gave the bail-out signal. (Co-pilot) Feldt and I managed to get it out of the spin and started to leave. As I got back on the flight deck, the top turret broke loose and pinned me to the floor. I saw the rest of the men ahead of me jumping and for the life of me I couldn't break loose from the turret, which weighs about 700 pounds. We were at 28,000 feet and I could feel myself passing out when there was a tremendous blast and sheet of flame.

When I came to I thought I must be dead, everything was so quiet. Then I realized that I was sailing through space. I immediately pulled my chute and then everything went dark again.

What happened to the best of my knowledge was that when I was still in the plane our bombs were hit and by some miracle of God I was blown free. As Wellbrock was being marched to a small outpost by a German soldier, he saw the bodies of Bob Sanders and three other soldiers.

Right waist gunner, William Voght, spoke of the crash in an interview with Army personnel after the war. *Just as I opened the bottom hatch to go out, the plane turned over, and instead of falling out of the bottom, I had to pull myself out, like going out a top exit. I think it threw (Sanders) and he was probably knocked out by a swinging waist gun.*[26]

Rob Sanders was fortunate. More information than he had hoped for poured in. It was actually overloading him with emotion and questions. The more information he found, the more he wanted. What were his uncle's last days like? Was there anyone who could talk with him about this man he never knew but who was so connected to his own life? Rob started taking care of himself, making sure he got enough sleep, jogging and trying to keep mentally strong enough to keep unraveling the threads of his uncle Bob's story. Rob was a firefighter and paramedic. He was accustomed to stress and to working under difficult conditions. But this was more than he had ever experienced and he had to work with the emotions brought up in him.

Bob Sanders was buried in the Ardennes American Cemetery in Neupre, Belgium. This information and the tragic story of his life was unknown to his family for nearly six decades. After all this time, Bob's nephew, who looked enough like him to be his twin, gave his life recognition and answered the unheard request of sixty years earlier.

Finally, Rob and Sharon approached the gates of the Ardennes American Cemetery. All the work they had done was coming together in a single moment. They were met by the cemetery superintendent, Hans Hooker, who had served as Alexander Haig's interpreter and chauffeur during the war.

> "... Rob knows the moment he has been waiting for most of his life has arrived. At the end of the long, tree-lined main drive stands a massive white limestone memorial and chapel with the distinctive eagle he has seen so many times in the literature Hooker has sent him. He knows that behind it are the graves of 5,328 servicemen killed in World War II, including his uncle, Robert W. Sanders.
>
> A matter of a few thousand yards away lies the body of the man he has connected with in such a special way over the last couple years – the man about whom he has dreamed all his life. In a matter of minutes, Rob will, in some sense, fulfill a part of his uncle's wish to come home. He will be the first one in his family to walk across this hallowed ground so far from the Cape his uncle loved and embrace Bob in spirit.

... Tucked under Rob's arm is the original box holding the folded American flag used to drape Bob's coffin when it was buried in Ardennes 52 years before. ...Kent had sent it with Rob to make the full circle back again to his brother's grave."[27]

When Rob explained that the flag had been in a trunk in his grandmother's attic, Hooker became silent with emotion. After a moment, with a wavering voice he asked, *Mr. Sanders, would you mind if we take our own flag down and put yours up?* Tears streamed down Rob's face as he saw the 48 star flag catch the wind and unfurl. Because the flag was so fragile, it was returned to Rob and he and Hooker folded it in military style. They returned to the car and continued their journey through the cemetery.

As Rob and Sharon drove through the cemetery, they looked at the sea of white marble crosses before them. Seen from the air, the crosses form a Greek cross which was used as a Christian symbol until the 8th or 9th century. Before Christianity, it was used as an emblem for Hecate, the Greek goddess of crossroads.

Soon, Rob and Sharon were standing in front of the grave of Robert W. Sanders:

"... The others fall back as Rob takes Sharon's hand and walks slowly to the cross. As he approaches, he embraces his wife with his left arm, burying his head in her neck and breaking into tears. His shoulders jerk, and for several minutes, the sadness he had carried for two generations of the Sanders family – sadness that was hidden away but never erased, never eased – was washed into the sacred ground of his uncle's grave.

... As the tears subside, he moves away from his wife, and she steps into the background. He kneels in prayer, clutching the cross with his right hand, for several minutes. He moves his head closer to the stone and rests his forehead on the center post of the cross. 'I apologized to him for taking so long.'

In his final act at the cross that day, Rob dips into his pocket and removes a small glass vial of Cape Cod Bay salt water and a small bag of beach sand he had collected at Ellis Landing in Brewster, near his uncle's beloved boyhood home. He sprinkles the water in front of the cross and rubs the sand into the base. Even though Bob had never been granted his last wish to come home from the war – 'dead or alive,' as he wrote to his mother – a part of Brewster had finally, after nearly 60 years, come home to him."[28]

Sharon Sanders had written a poem in honor of her husband's uncle, Robert W. Sanders, and recited it at the service given for him in the chapel at the Ardennes American Cemetery. During the service she stepped forward and through her poem, *The Final Mission*, spoke what she believed to be the message of Bob Sanders spirit.

The Final Mission

My face is just a memory
That chapter had once been closed
Since now the book is reopened
A story destined to be told.

Life presents its challenges
God knows I had a few
Offering several directions
Choices always up to you.

I walked my path a proud man
Willing to accept my fate
So when duty called upon me
I did not hesitate.

My pride with home and family
Was a daily aching yearn
Hoping maybe someday
God would guide my safe return.

Not knowing mission fifty
Would be my final flight
The angels came to greet me
To escort me through the light.

My body lies in Belgium
At rest on sacred ground
My brother lay beside me
God's peace we finally found.

I had hoped to set example
To those I had left behind
My presence always with you
Within your heart and mind.

We've drawn our own conclusions
To death and afterlife
Denial to protect us
From our personal sacrifice.

Surrender your tears and anger
To accept the cards at hand
I promise there will come a day
You will finally understand.

My message here is simple
There is nothing more to say
For all to walk on forward
We must heal yesterday.

Pray for love and forgiveness
For that is the ultimate plan
Embrace your life and each other
So we can walk hand in hand.

The War On Terror

Sadly, war is a pervasive part of our history. On September 11, 2001, terror struck every American and overwhelming pain filled every heart as people listened to news that a Boeing 767 had flown into the north tower of the World Trade Center in New York City at 8:45 a.m. American Airlines flight 11 had left Boston's Logan Airport for Los Angeles at 7:59 that Tuesday morning with eighty-one passengers and eleven crew members aboard. As more television sets were turned on to see what had happened, people watched in horror as another Boeing 767 flew into the south tower of the World Trade Center at 9:06 a.m. United Airlines flight 175 had left Boston's Logan Airport for Los Angeles with fifty-six passengers and nine crew aboard that morning at 7:58 a.m.

Overwhelmed by emotions of fear, horror and confusion at what they were seeing, people watched frozen in time as they heard that yet another plane, American Airlines flight

77, had hit the west side of the Pentagon at 9:40 a.m. At 8:10 a.m. that same Tuesday morning, the Boeing 757 had departed Washington Dulles Airport for Los Angeles with fifty-eight passengers and six crew members aboard. People, as stunned and confused as they were, understood that what they were seeing was no accident.

The American people, numb, with tears flowing, watched as the two towers that symbolized economic strength and prosperity, collapsed in fire and smoke. People began calling friends and relatives. For some, it brought back memories of Pearl Harbor. At 10:37 a.m., United Airlines flight 93 crashed in Shanksville, Pennsylvania, brought down by heroic passengers willing to sacrifice their own lives to prevent the plane from striking yet another building.

Time Magazine, described the reaction on Capitol Hill:

"... At 7:30 p.m. Tuesday, with the Pentagon still in flames, the congressional leadership, with a crowd of Senators and Congressmen behind them, stood on the Capitol steps. 'When Americans suffer and when people perpetrate acts against this country, we as a Congress and as a government stand united, and stand together,' said an angry Dennis Hastert, Speaker of the House, with Democrat Dick Gephardt standing stony silent beside him. Both parties 'will stand shoulder to shoulder to fight this evil,' Hastert promised. He asked everyone to bow their heads in a moment of silence. Afterward the Congressmen and Senators, Republicans hugging Democrats, broke out into a chorus of *God Bless America.*"[29]

The day that was a nightmare was simply termed *9/11*. The nation bonded together in patriotism, people contributing whatever they could to help those in need.

Entertainers raised funds for victims and their families. Singers and musicians performed in a Telethon fund-raiser which brought in $100 million to assist those in need.

Cape Cod joined others in responding to the call for help. In an article entitled, *Cape doctor answers call for help*, the *Cape Cod Times* described how Dr. John Jardine of Falmouth, an emergency room physician, drove to Newburgh, New York, joining nurses and technicians also trained in emergency treatment. Dr. Jardine was surprised when he was unable to treat many victims as they were buried under debris from the falling buildings. His patients were mostly rescue workers who had been hurt in the line of duty or who were having respiratory problems from breathing air filled with debris. Dr. Jardine was not alone. Many physicians and firefighters left the Cape to help in New York City.

On September 13, 2001, headlines on the front page of *The Register* read *Take a moment and pray for our country.*

"... Otis Air Base still stood at 'high alert'. On Tuesday, F-15 fighter interceptor aircraft were taking off from there for New York to help inspect the skies in the wake of nation's worst-ever act of terrorism ... Across Cape Cod, thousands woke up Wednesday to contemplate a world that never will be the same again, and to consider how in any small way they could show their sympathy and patriotism."

MA Search and Rescue Team at the World Trade Center, New York City

Photo by Robert Scott Button; Photo courtesy of *The Register*.

Julie Sweeney, a teacher in the Dennis-Yarmouth High School, lost her husband, Brian, killed when United Airlines flight 175 crashed into the World Trade Center. Brian had tried to call her from the hijacked airplane. When he did not reach her, he called his mother to tell her what was happening aboard his flight. Friends and neighbors looked for ways to help not only Julie but also others they knew who had lost a friend or family member.

The Register reported that:

"... Six Cape Cod firefighters from Yarmouth, Hyannis, and Sandwich, were at the disaster scene Wednesday morning after driving to New York City late Tuesday. They are part of the Urban Search and Rescue Team operating out of Beverly, which was the first of 27 such teams in the nation to reach the disaster scene.

For most Cape Codders unable to contribute directly, there was blood to give at Red Cross locations or Cape Cod and Falmouth hospitals. So strong was the rush to give blood that officials Wednesday were encouraging people to wait until at least Thursday to come in."

On September 20, 2001, *The Register* displayed the headlines, *Courage is beaming at 'Ground Hero'*. This article described six rescuers from Cape Cod who helped in the aftermath of the attack:

"Less than three hours after the twin towers of the World Trade Center had collapsed in and incredulous roar of fire and dust, the six Cape Cod rescue workers were speeding to New York City.

All the years of training, all the experience, all the courage, however, couldn't begin to prepare them for the apocalyptic vision of ground zero. Tens of thousands of tons of concrete reduced to ash, as though a volcano had erupted.

... Even on Sunday, days after the last of so few survivors had been pulled from the ungodly wreckage, Sandwich firefighter Scott Ames remained stalwart. 'We still hold out hope.'

... More than 5,000 people missing; more than 200 firefighters among them. So, as the Cape Codders stepped across the simmering rubble, as they clawed and scraped away the debris, the numbers glared at them.

... Team leader and Hyannis Fire Department Lieutenant Thomas Kenney worked the day shift with West Barnstable Firefighter Jim Murphy. Scott Ames, Yarmouth Firefighter Robert Reardon, and Hyannis firefighters Chris Standish and Brett Grandaw worked the night shift.

... 110 stories – two buildings – not even there,' Kenney said, still awestruck after days at ground zero.

If you leveled Main Street in Hyannis east to west it wouldn't be as big as this is. The Cape Cod Mall and the Hyannis K-Mart Plaza together would not even come close to filling it, he said."[30]

"Ground Hero"
Hyannis Fire Lt. Thomas Kenney stands in the middle of what was the World Trade Center
Photo by Robert Scott Button; Photo courtesy of *The Register*.

While rescuers from Cape Cod worked in New York City, teachers on Cape Cod worked at home with their students. The *Cape Cod Times,* in an article entitled *Learning about tragedy,* told of a student in the ninth grade who asked his teacher if he noticed that the date *9/11* could also be looked at as 911, the nationally used emergency telephone number. In school, students asked questions, considered consequences of action taken, and compared responses to the World Trade Center attack and the Pearl Harbor attack. Even though it seemed as if this was America's saddest hour, students heard encouragement and were given a positive outlook. As one teacher put it, *Most people are decent and good. Americans will come together … There is goodness in the world and that will prevail.*

Cape Cod businesses joined in an effort to help victims, families, and rescuers of this national disaster. Restaurants gave a day's profit as donation. Canisters were put on counters for donations and profits from specified services were donated. Patriotism ran high with the American flag displayed in front of houses, shops and across bridges.

Everyone pulled together to do what they could but an underlying fear pervaded the country. Fear that there would be another attack. Fear that there would be a slump in the economy and fear of flying.

Economic Response
As has happened so many times throughout Cape Cod's history, the hardest hit of the Cape's industries was the fishing industry. According to the *Cape Cod Times*:

> … the terrorist attacks may have hurt fishing as much as any local business. Prices dropped after the attacks

because business dropped at the 'white tablecloth' restaurants in New York City, Boston and Philadelphia that typically buy from Cape Cod fishermen.

Today, as we enter 2003, our national strength and resolve is again strong as we deal with national threats and difficulties.

---

[1] Warren, James. Letter to Mercy Otis Warren, 18 June 1775. Warren-Adams Papers, Massachusetts Historical Society.

[2] Cape Cod Its People and Their History, Henry C. Kittredge, page 257.

[3] Cape Cod Its People and Their History, Henry C. Kittredge, page 257, 258.

[4] Cape Cod Its People and Their History, henry C. Kittredge, page 261.

[5] Reminiscences Of Three Years' Service In The Civil War, By A Cape Cod Boy, John J. Ryder, page 27, 28.

[6] Reminiscences Of Three Years' Service In The Civil War, By A Cape Cod Boy, John J. Ryder, page 39.

[7] Reminiscences Of Three Years' Service In The Civil War, By A Cape Cod Boy, John J. Ryder, page 40.

[8] The Town Of Yarmouth, Massachusetts: A History, 1639-1989, Marion Vuilleumier, page 70, 71.

[9] Cape Cod Times, U-boat attack!, Mike Iaacuessa, November 10, 1991, article..

[10] Time And The Town – A Provincetown Chronicle, Mary Heaton Vorse, page 133.

[11] Time And The Town – A Provincetown Chronicle, Mary Heaton Vorse, page 133, 134.

[12] Private interview With Mr. Basil Dandison, May 17, 2002. Sadly, Mr. Basil Dandison died on January 4, 2003 prior to publication of this work.

[13] The Town Of Yarmouth, Massachusetts: A History, 1639-1989, Marion Vuilleumier, page 117, 118.

[14] The Town Of Yarmouth, Massachusetts: A History, 1639-1989, Marion Vuilleumier, page 120.

[15] Camp Edwards Is Completed, Captain Fred E. Brake, Q.M.C., article.

[16] The Register, The Moments That Mattered, December 30, 1999, The Upper Cape Codder, article.

[17] Camp Edwards Is Completed, Captain Fred E. Brake, Q.M.C, article.

[18] The Register, The Moments That Mattered, December 30, 1999, The Upper Cape Codder, article.

[19] Cape Cod Times, Kevin Dennehy, June 2, 2002, article.

[20] Falmouth Enterprise, April 12, 1946, article.

[21] Ambergris And Arrowheads: Growing up on Cape Cod In the 1930s0s and 1940s, Anne N. Harmon, page 95.

[22] Ambergris And Arrowheads: Growing Up on Cape Cod In the 1930s and 1940s, Anne N. Harmon, page 101.

[23] Cape Cod Times, Remembering Pearl Harbor, Robin Lord, article.

[24] Cape Cod Times, Robin Lord, May 23, 2001, article.

[25] Cape Cod Times, Robin Lord, May, 2001, article.
[26] Cape Cod Times, Robin Lord, June, 2001, article.
[27] Cape Cod Times, Robin Lord, June, 2001, article.
[28] Cape Cod Times, Robin Lord, June, 2001, article.
[29] Time Magazine, September 11, 2001, article.
[30] The Register, Courage is beaming at 'Ground Hero', Karen Monahan, September 20, 2001, article.

CHAPTER 6:
SURVIVAL

Native Cape Codders

When Europeans arrived on Cape Cod in the 1600s, they were met by Wampanoags, (wäm′ p☐ nō′ ag) referred to as *Native People.* Approximately thirty tribes were members of the Wampanoag Indian Federation that stretched from Cape Cod to Rhode Island. Wampag means bright light. These are the people of the east and their name, Wampanoag, means People of the Dawn, or People of the First Light. According to Kittredge:

> "All Cape Indians belonged nominally to the Wampanoags, but thanks to the geographical isolation of the Cape, each little tribe – and there were half a dozen or more of them – was free to go its own gait under its own sachem. …They were independent, peace-loving, and non-progressive. At Falmouth were the Succonessitts. The tribe that lived in and near Sandwich called themselves Manomets; those at Barnstable and Yarmouth were Mattakees and Cummaquids; the Monomoyicks occupied what is now Chatham; the Nausets controlled Eastham, and the northernmost group, who lived in the neighborhood of Truro, were called Pamets."[1]

Fishing, planting, harvesting and hunting were the way of life for each Wampanoag community. All members of a community had the right to use all land as no one person owned land to the exclusion of others. Each family used a particular piece of land designated by the Sachem (chief) and his council. In gratitude, some of the harvest was given to the Sachem. In 1620, as Plymouth Plantation was being settled, Massasoit was the highest Sachem of the Wampanoags.

Wampanoag custom was to build lodging in many areas and stay in different places according to the season. When and where food was plentiful dictated where a dwelling was built and when a family lived there.

The arrival of Europeans in the 1600s disrupted the Wampanoags' way of life. Sometimes things went well and gifts were exchanged. Other times interactions were hostile. An early hostile exchange occurred during John Smith's visit to Cape Cod in 1614. Smith was mapping the coast of what is now New England and as he departed for England, his lieutenant, Thomas Hunt, kidnapped twenty-seven Wampanoag men and sold them as slaves in Spain. Later, in 1616, when a French vessel was wrecked on the shores of Cape Cod, survivors were taken prisoner and forced to act as servants within Wampanoag communities.

More devastating to Wampanoags than these hostile episodes was the plague of 1618. This plague, a form of typhus that exists in unclean living conditions, was brought to the Cape by Europeans. The plague destroyed whole villages and killed in the vicinity of seventy percent of the Wampanoag population of Southeastern Massachusetts. Weakened by these losses, Massasoit was forced to submit to Canonicus, Sachem of the Narragansett, thereby making Canonicus the region's most powerful Sachem. This was devastating to Massasoit as he and his father a generation earlier had warred with the Narragansett.

Arrival of the English presented an opportunity for Massasoit to re-establish strength and reputation among his people. In March, 1621, he signed a peace treaty with the Pilgrims which gave him both physical strength from British men and arms and the opportunity for enhanced trade. In 1623, after Edward Winslow of the Plymouth Plantation helped him recover from an illness that had blinded him and might well have taken his life, Massasoit warned the colonists of an impending attack which was then successfully prevented. Based on the treaty of 1621, Massasoit remained neutral during the Pequot war of 1636.

Wampanoag communities were crowded into ever smaller areas as more Europeans arrived on Cape Cod. Different approaches to land ownership and use created problems between settlers and Native Peoples. Wampanoags were prevented from moving to alternative living areas with seasonal changes. Animals that settlers brought, including pigs and cows, ruined crops planted by Wampanoags. And again, another illness brought by Europeans ravaged both Native People and English settlers. Small pox destroyed many indigenous communities throughout the western hemisphere.

Praying Indians

When settlers arrived and began communicating with Native People, they found a belief system in some ways much like their own and in other ways quite different.

"Two major gods, it seems, presided over the Indian destinies. The greater of these they called Kiehtan. He was their creator and the creator of all else besides, earth and sea, sky and stars. The naturalness of the Adam and Eve story as an explanation for man's existence on the earth is strikingly illustrated by the Indian idea that Kiehtan had first created one man and one woman from whom they all were descended. Kiehtan lived in heaven, and to him went the spirits of all the dead; to be admitted if they had been good; otherwise to be sentenced to a wretched and restless existence of aimless wandering in a sort of Cimmerian fog."[2]

Native People used regional stories similar to European myths to explain circumstances. One example is the story of Maushop, a benevolent giant, believed to be the originator of fog. Kittredge describes the fable:

"... Long years before, they said, a huge bird used to visit the shores of Yarmouth and carry off the children in its talons, flying with them to the south out over Vineyard Sound. Maushop, a benevolent giant of Yarmouth, at last grew tired of this procedure and decided to pursue the bird and kill it. So, on its next appearance, he followed it out across the Sound, wading along as fast as he could, until finally, pretty well exhausted, he reached an unknown island on the other side, where he found a huge tree piled about with the bones of children. 'It is time for a smoke,' said Maushop to himself, and reached for his tobacco. But he had forgotten to bring any with him and was obliged to use poke instead – a plant which he found growing plentifully on the island. This poke he puffed with such effect that the whole Sound and the shores on both sides of it were enveloped with the smoke; and forever after when a fog settled down over the south shore of the Cape, the Indians would nod wisely and say, 'There's old Maushop smoking his pipe."[3]

When settlers arrived, they began converting Wampanoags to Christianity with many ministers taking on this task. But two people, Richard Bourne and Samuel Treat, also helped Wampanoags become more independent.

Richard Bourne established himself in Sandwich in 1641. He was not a minister but he moved to Sandwich in order to help Native People establish a government of their own and a community on land of their own. By 1665, Wampanoags could hold their own courts and try criminals. They had also received title to fifty square miles of land in Mashpee. At the same time that Bourne worked to promote self sufficiency among the tribes, he preached Christianity. He reported that with the assistance of four already converted Native People as preaching assistants, he was able to convert five hundred people living in Mashpee. In 1670, he was ordained as minister of the church in Mashpee and remained in his ministry until his death in 1685.

Native People who converted to Christianity were known as *Praying Indians.* What bonded Native People to settlers, however, was not so much religion but rather the peoples' devotion to leaders such as Richard Bourne and Samuel Treat, another minister who helped Bourne in his effort. This devotion was one reason why one of the most devastating wars of the time was not fought on Cape Cod soil.

King Philip's War

Massasoit had two sons. The eldest was Wamsutta, called Alexander by the English, and the second was Metacom whose English name was Philip[p]. When

---

[p] Based on treaties signed between 1639 and 1662, there is controversy as to whether Wamsutta and Metacom were indeed brothers and whether Metacom was Massasoit's son or grandson. For additional information see http://members.aol.com/calebj/massasoit.html and *New England Historic and Genealogical Register* 144:211-214.

Massasoit died in approximately 1660, Wamsutta became Sachem. In 1662, the Plymouth government summoned Wamsutta to question him about charges that he was selling land promised by Plymouth to others. During his stay in Plymouth, Wamsutta became ill. When he died shortly after returning home, Metacom became Sachem. It wasn't long before he, too, was summoned to Plymouth to address rumors that Native People were plotting against the English.

These rumors began in response to increasing hostility of Native Peoples toward settlers as Native People were obliged to sell land in order to purchase English goods. Tensions between settlers and Native People subsided for a short time but soon increased again. The English did not trust Metacom and in 1671, when colonial rangers discovered a band of armed Native men, the Plymouth government mandated that Native People surrender their guns. When confrontations continued, Metacom was forced to sign a new treaty which gave the English government control over his people.

In January, 1675, the murder of John Sassamon, a Christian Indian who had been serving the English as an informer, brought the two communities to the brink of war. There was suspicion that Metacom had commissioned the execution and a witness identified three Wampanoag men as the killers. Tried under English jurisdiction because John Sassamon was Christian and therefore considered an English subject, the three Wampanoags were executed.

Then, with an incident in June, 1675, war began. Upon arriving home, a colonist shot and killed a Native man he saw running from his house. Native People responded with a revenge attack in which several English people were killed. Plymouth, Massachusetts Bay and the Connecticut Colonies joined together to fight Metacom while Native People from tribes as far away as the Hudson River joined Metacom. The war had spread to the Connecticut river valley.

The Narragansett, a neutral nation, were accused by the colonists of acting in bad faith when they harbored fugitives. Given this provocation, one thousand colonial soldiers attacked the unsuspecting Narragansett in December, 1675. Many Natives were killed and their fort burned causing the Narragansett to join Metacom in the war.

Native People had been driven from their communities, had lost their cornfields and had been denied land on which to hunt for food. This, along with a harsh winter, led Natives to raid English farming communities for food and supplies. Many Natick, Ponkapoag and Mattakeeset people were interred on Deer Island in Boston Harbor and Clark's Island in Plymouth Harbor to prevent them from aiding the enemy.

Native People on Cape Cod took a different stand when it came to joining Metacom. They were not disposed to follow King Philip, as the English called Metacom, and fight against people who had in many ways helped them secure land and taught them to form their own government. Conflicts between Native People and the English were not as severe on Cape Cod as elsewhere.

Kittredge wrote:

> "... The condition of the Cape during this war, though actually a very happy one, was potentially critical. As long as the Cape Indians refused to join Philip or listen to his

anti-white propaganda, the settlers there were in a far better position than the other colonists. King Philip was not in their vicinity, and it was unlikely that any fighting would take place on Cape soil."[4]

Native People living on Cape Cod stood by their convictions; some even enlisted in the settlers' army and fought against their own people. Captain Benjamin Church of Plymouth Colony led one of the English ranger companies. These small groups of both Native and English rangers supported larger armies. Native soldiers were most helpful in advising their colonial commanders of strategies that would lead them to the enemy. Ranger companies, combined with larger English armies, wore down Metacom's resistance and that of his allies causing many Natives to join the English. Participation of Native soldiers in English armies was instrumental in allowing the English to succeed in this war.

Native resistance ended by the end of summer in 1676. Many tribes were captured or surrendered. Some Native People left to find refuge in Maine or New York. Others were sold as slaves. Metacom was killed in Mount Hope, Rhode Island, by a Native who had joined colonists commanded by Captain Benjamin Church. His head was placed on a pole in Plymouth as was the custom of the settlers. His wife and son were captured, sold into slavery and taken to Bermuda.

Why would Native People of Cape Cod respond so differently from those from other areas? Their response showed their devotion and gratitude to missionaries Richard Bourne and Samuel Treat. Another reason they did not become involved in the war was that they were tired. They were tired from the plague of 1618 and tired after arrival of Europeans forced them to change their customs and way of living. Eventually, after being

crowded off the land they had always known and succumbing to the small pox epidemic, they watched their population decrease to only a scattered few by 1764.

King Philip's War was not a great a victory for the English. It caused economic depression and was one of the most costly wars in American history in terms of human life. For Native People it was devastating. When the settlers arrived there were approximately 40,000 Wampanoags in southeastern Massachusetts. Plagues from 1614 to 1620 reduced their numbers to 12,000 and the war took another 3,000. Nearly 80 percent of the Native population had died. Native People of Cape Cod managed to survive by accepting change without losing their own identity and today continue their oral and cultural traditions.

Hands Outstretched

Consequences of King Philip's War extended far beyond continental North America as Native People were sold into slavery on the British island of Bermuda. What became of these people and how they were connected to those who remained in New England has long been of interest. Recently, the *Cape Cod Times* printed a story entitled *Worlds Rejoined* by Paula Peters. Could it be that ancestors of Native People who were sold into slavery and transported to Bermuda had connected with their homeland? Because there are no papers recording genealogy, reconnection is based on oral history of individual families. Peters' story is about two men. One was raised in both Charleston, Rhode Island and Mashpee, Massachusetts. He is Annawon Weeden, 26, named after the last Wampanoag warrior to surrender to the colonial army after King Philip's War in 1676. His father was Pequot and his mother Wampanoag. ... *Those are both strong Indian communities, and my parents gave me traditional values, and my Indian pride has been instilled in me since day one,* Weeden explained. The other man, Ian Pitcher, 36, was raised on St. David's Island in Bermuda. Even though there was little of his native culture on the Island, Ian knew the stories that linked him to Native People in America.

Annawon Weeden and Ian Pitcher met while attending a four-day cultural exchange held on St. David's Island. Weeden could trace his Wampanoag and Pequot heritage to the period of both King Philip's War and the Pequot War.

The Pequots occupied the territory now known as southeastern Connecticut. They were the first tribe to resist colonial encroachment and subjugation. When a colonial captain was killed, the Pequots refused to surrender those responsible for the killing and war with the colonists ensued in 1636. The Massachusetts, Plymouth and Connecticut colonies, allied with the Narragansett tribe, fought against the Pequots. Massasoit and the Wampanoags of southeastern Massachusetts did not participate in this war.

The war ended in May, 1637, when colonial troops surrounded the Pequot position at Mystic, Connecticut. They set the village on fire and killed nearly seven hundred Pequots, including women and children. This loss, along with the loss of four thousand to small pox in 1633, reduced the Pequot population by nearly 60 percent from an estimated number of 8,000. The surviving Pequots were taken as slaves or forced to accept Christianity.

Annawon Weeden has held tight to his native traditions. He traced his ancestors to a Pequot named Major Simons who, as a mercenary during King Philip's War, was paid to fight with the English against Metacom. When the war ended, Mashpee, Annawon Weeden's town, was a village of Christian or *Praying Indians* and these people were not harmed.

Pitcher's great-great grandmother was Susannah Lowe, born in 1844. It is through her that Pitcher is connected to Metacom's wife, Wootenekunooski. His story, told through generations, answers the question of what became of Wootenekunooski, and her son. It is believed that Wootenekunooski married an African slave and became matriarch of the Minors family on St. David's Island. Stuart Hollis, a descendent of the Minors family, has researched his family's heritage.

"... The Indian queen's descendants include a slave named Susannah, who passed on the story of her royal ancestry to a young Bermudan boy named Outerbridge in the early 1800s. She was an elderly woman at the time, but told the boy she was a princess descended from the Indian King Philip."[5]

JOURNEY TO BERMUDA

1609 - Members of the Powatan tribe in Virginia become first indians sold into slavery in Bermuda.

1620 - Bermuda colony helps fund Mayflower expedition, and Pil-

Massasoit, at right, brings food to the early European settlers of New England.

grim separatists settle colony at Plymouth.

1621 - Ousamequin, who was Massasoit, or supreme leader, of the Wampanoag, signs friendship treaty with English settlers.

1637 - Pequot War against colonists ends with massacre of 400 to 700 Indians at Mystic, Conn.

1644 - Unknown number of Pequot prisoners of war enslaved and shipped to Bermuda.

1661 - Ousamequin dies and is succeeded by oldest son, Wamsutta.

1662 - Wamsutta dies suspiciously after a visit to colony at Plymouth and is succeeded by

Metacom, called King Philip by the English.

1675 - King Philip's War erupts after years of Indian resistance to colonization.

1676 - Metacom is killed at Mount Hope, R.I., ending the war.

1677 - Metacom's wife and son enslaved and sent to Bermuda.

1678 - As many as 80 Indian men, believed to be prisoners of King Philip's War, are shipped to Bermuda and purchased by Capt. Anthony White, the colony's largest land holder.

Worlds Rejoined
by Paula Peters, Courtesy of *Cape Cod Times*

Centuries of unrecorded marriages, deaths and slave births were kept alive through oral histories. Information handed down through these stories showed the connection. Annawon Weeden and Ian Pitcher appear to be a link that connects those on St. David's Island in Bermuda to Native People of southeastern Massachusetts. Finally, long lost relatives, split apart by more than 1,000 miles of sea, reached out and shook hands with one another.

[1] Cape Cod Its People and Their History, Henry C. Kittredge, page28.
[2] Cape Cod Its People and Their History, Henry C. Kittredge, page 40.
[3] Cape Cod Its People and Their History, Henry C. Kittredge, page 42.
[4] Cape Cod Its People and Their History, Henry C. Kittredge, page 46.
[5] Cape Cod Times, Worlds rejoined, Paula Peters, July 13, 2002, article.

Epilogue

Throughout Cape Cod's history, the symbiotic relationship of people who choose to live here and the land itself is evident. Only a certain kind of person is attracted to such a place. Nothing here stays the same. This land gives and it takes away. People who call themselves Cape Codders wear the name proudly, for they are aware that change is part of that definition and to remain here means that they must always be ready to adapt to a place that will not remain the same. Even the land will not remain the same. It will change year by year, month by month, even day by day.

People who call Cape Cod home are as ever changing as the land. They become involved with town activities, research town histories and even start new careers. Change is the attraction. It is what bonds place and person. Change is challenge and Cape Codders thrive on it. As the land has weathered storms, so have the people. People of this land have evolved with the changing needs of the fishing industry, cranberry industry and tourism. As the land changes and evolves, so do the people who have chosen Cape Cod as home. We are a reflection of the land.

Appendices

Appendix A: Packet Ship Advertisement

From Montreal Gazette, June 14, 1834

New York and Liverpool Packets

The subscribers have established the following ships as a LINE OF PACKETS between this port and Liverpool, to leave New York on the 14th, and Liverpool on the 30th of each month.

	From (New York)	From (Liverpool)
New Ship St Andrew, J. Taubman, Master.	June 14	July 20
	Oct 14	Nov 30
	Feb 14	Mar 30
Ship Howard, T.M. Hervey, jr., Master	July 14	Aug 30
	Nov 14	Dec 30
	Mar 14	April 30
Ship Ajax, C.A. Hiern, Master	Aug 14	Sep 30
	Dec 14	Jan 30
	April 14	May 30
Ship St. George, W.C. Thomson, Master	Sept 14	Oct 30
	Jan 14	Feb 28
	May 14	June 30

The above packets are ships of the first class, coppered and copper fastened. The greatest exertions will be made to promote the interests of importers, by the speedy and safe delivery of their goods. Nothing has been omitted in the construction and furniture of their cabins, which can contribute to the comfort of Passangers. The price of passage in the cabin is fixed at one hundred and ten dolars, or one hundred and forty dollars for the exclusive use of a state-room by one passenger. Wines and stores of the best quality provided without additional charge.

The days of sailing will be punctually observed. For freight or passage, apply to the masters, on board, to
STEPHEN WHITNEY,
GRACIE PRIME & Co., or
ROBERT KERMIT,
74, South street.
New York, May 15, 1834.

Appendix B: Ellen M. Knights' Letter

Brig COLORADO - Harbor of Valparaiso - March 31 1850

Mr. I.E. Sanborn Dear Sir,

The Captain of the Ship Pacific of Boston has promised to take a pacage [sic] of letters for us to New York. I write to inform you of our safety and my uninterupted [sic] good health. I was a little sea sick for two days, have never been confined to my birth [sic] a whole day since I left Boston. Weigh two hundred and five lbs. I am in good spirits. I like Capt. Baker very much. We have singing and prayers morning and evening and a sermon every Sabbath, when the weather will permit. When two weeks out of Boston we established a weekly paper to be made up of original matter contributed by the passengers. Communications handed to Mr. F.H. Woods, The Editor where copied in to a large Book and the "Boston & California Pioneer" was read to us every Tuesday Evening. Advertisements of Lectures Concerts, Hat Stores, Shoe Stores. Lost Children, Patriotic, Moral and Religious peaces [sic], appear most every week. 4 or 5 Poets Some very good, some good for nothing. In our Police reports one week we were informed that "Sam'l M. Braclett was fined five dollars for whipping one of his children". We have enjoyed ourselves vary [sic] well, had vary [sic] little sickness of any kind. Pleasant weather from Boston to St. Catherines visiting the different Calafornia [sic] vessells [sic] and the natives on Shore. Dined at the Consuls Mr. Cathcart who was formerly an old whaleman from Nantucket, has married a native and has a large family of children, has resided there 22 years. Sailed from St. Catherines the 2nd of January. 1 Ship I Bark 1 Brig and 2 Schon's [Schooners!] came out in company with us All California bound; they all out sailed us; had a pleasant run down the coast of Brazil went inside the Falkland Islands but did not see land till we made Staten land the 25th Jan., 14 sail in sight some of which were whalers. Jan. 28th made Cape Horn. Jan. 30th commenced with light winds from S E (our true course was west). At 10am wind S W increasing to a gale. At 4pm Coast of Terra del Fuego on our lea 15 miles distant; our only chance was now in carying [sic] sail. At 9pm away went Jib Boom, Foretopmast and Maintopgallant mast, blowing a gale all the while. Anxiety and alarm was in every countanance. [sic] The Sailors dared not go aloft to cut away the broken spars. Capt. Baker Said if It was "God will we should go clear If not York Minster Cape would bring us up before morning, he had done all he could". The Passengers looked on in Silence while the Capt. and Mate consulted maps and charts. It was a long and sleepless night for us all. At daylight we had passed the cape, how near we could not exactly tell but we where [sic] close in to land, the wind favored us 2 points we tacked ship and stood out to sea, thankfull [sic] enough for plenty of sea room. When we where [sic] a hundred miles or so from land, we lay too [sic] and when the gale was over cleared up the wreck. We where [sic] five weeks beating about with gale after gale--what we gained one day we lost the next by laying too. [sic] February 26th Lattitude [sic] 530 43 South Longitude 770 30, Capt. Baker united in Marriage Mr. Job Henry Grush of Roxbury and Miss Mary Jane Stinchfield. The parties were not acquainted before coming on board. The Capt. published them at Morning Prayers. Excitement and curiosity privailed [sic] for the intended wedding was known to but few. Jokes passed. Love, Courtship and Marriage was talked of. The morning was spent in moving beds, boxes trunks, and preparing a room for the Bride. At 4 O'Clock pm the bride and groom made the appearance neatly dressed. Mr. Woods of Boston and myself had the honor of standing up with them. The gong was rung. The gentlemen Passengers came out on this Occasion in fancy costume, different nations fashions trades Shapes and Colours where [sic] represented--most all wore enormous paper collars, Small men where [sic] stuffed to twice there [sic] usual size. Swords, Pistols, Eppiletts [sic] Guns, rings, eyeglasses, Tartan plaids and Policemen with badges where [sic] all there, while the representative from Sweet Irelande [sic] keept [sic] the door with a Shelalah [sic] in his hand. Perfect order was maintained while the marriage ceremony was read and prayer offered, then came kisses and congratulations for the Bride and nine hearty cheers for the groom. An extra supper was provided. At midnight they where [sic] serenaded by the Owl Club of which Mr. Grush was a member--thus ended our Cape Horn wedding--a time that will long be remembered by us all--we all thought that such an important event would bring us a fair wind. It came a few days after and we had a good run to this port--Arrived here the 14th March. A whole fleet of vessells [sic] came in with us. All the vessells [sic] we left at St. Catherines have been here and gone, before we arrived. It will take about 3 weeks to repair the damage done the vessell [sic] and get fresh provision and water-- we shall be ready to sail the first fair wind after today. The Ship Sunden and Charlotte of Boston are here from California. Vessells [sic] are coming here from there most every week. They do not give the place a vary [sic] good name. The worst place for gambling and drinking in the world. They arae bringing the sick from California here. Men stop at the diggings till the wet season and they get worn out and then ship for a run down the coast--living on Salt Provision so ling at the mines they have the scurvy in a little time--one ship came in with only 2 well men--all sick with scurvy. Bitter complaints are made of the American Hospital here. It certainly is a most miserable place. The sailors say It is shure [sic] death to a man to go there. It is owned by Dr. Page, a Massachusetts man said to be worth 50 or 60 thousand doll[ar]s. We found Mr. Johnson one of our company at the English Hospital--he pays 4 dollars per day and has good care and attendance. He came here in Reindeer • from Boston is improveing [sic] in health. The E Hospital is well conducted, receives government patronage-our government ought to do something for ours--vegetables and fruit are very scarce in California. The report here is that Mr. Moorhouse late American Consul and 2 other gentlemen have bought up all the Flour and fresh provisions at Conseption [sic] for one year--for the California markett. [sic] Mr. Moorhouse has gone to California. 1 gentleman remains here and 1 goes to Conception--prices fixed on a sliding scale--I presume you understand how these speculation in lying up Flour Mills as managed. [T]he latest dates I have seen is the New York Herald of Jan. 14th we were shocked at the news of Dr. Parkmas death and the arrest of Proff. Webster. Mr. Potter the present American Consul is a pleasant gentlemanly man, he was at the Law School at Cambridge 10 or 12 years since. Postage on letters from here to New York only 75 cts. I like Valparaiso vary [sic] much--the city is built at the foot of a range of mountains while towering above them is the lofty Andes. The principal trade is in the hands of English and American men. Every thing is high but fruit and vegetables those are plenty and fine. Potatoes and onions and quinces are superior to any I ever saw in the States. Apples, Pears, Peaches, Appricotts [sic], Figs, Oranges, Lemons, Limes, Grapes and other things plenty and cheap. Horses are plenty and beautiful I [sic], every body rides on horseback--much of the labor is done by mules. Horse racing and Theatrical Amusements on Sunday. The Spanish and Chilean women never wear any Bonnetts [sic]--most of them smoke cigars. We visited the Fort was politely rec'd by the Officers--treated to cake, wine and cigars. Last Friday eve we were invited to an entertainment on board the Helen S. Page from Boston--we had music, dancing and Singing and a splendid supper. The Marcia Cleaves from Boston arrived yesterday. I suppose you would like to know If I have ever repented starting for California-To tell the truth, the night we expected to go ashore on the Coast of "Terra del Fuego" I wished myself anywhere but where I was--at no other time have I regretted It for a moment. I have written this in a hurry as I did not know of the opportunity to send till within a few hours--I have no time to copy or correct. Please excuse my poor scholarship and do not expose my ignorance to any but my friends. My letter to Nancy went on last weeks Steamer. I send one to my Father with this. I hope your family and all my friends are well. Mrs. Brackett wishes to be affectionately remembered to Mr. & Mrs. Harris, is well and does not regrett [sic] starting for California. will write to Mr. Harris folks when we arrive at California. My respects to all kind friends that inquire after me, Peticularly [sic] Mr. Cruft. with manny [sic] thanks to you and Mrs.

Sanborn for all your kindnesses to me and mine and the wish that every good may attend you -- I am you friend -- Ellen M. Knights

There is no place like New England. I hope to lay my bones in soil yet

- Reindeer - John Lord, Master - sailed from Boston 1849-11-22 - arrived at San Francisco 1850-04-02 :- Reported 122 days net, and 38 days from Valparaiso, claimed as a record.
- Reindeer - John Lord, Master - 800.26:156.6 x 33.5 x 22 - built by Donald McKay, East Boston, launched 1849-06-09 - owned by J.M. Forbes, Geo. B. Upton & Sampson & Tappan, Boston (wrecked in South Seas, 1859-02-12)

Appendix C: Victorian Games

Blind Man's Bluff

At a party, one child is blindfolded while the others scatter and after a count, remain still. The blindfolded child wanders about until he or she touches another child. The blindfolded child then attempts to identify the child found. If correct, the blindfold passes to the named child. If wrong, the blindfolded child tries once more. If wrong a second time, he or she names the next person to be blindfolded.

Hunt the Thimble

At a party, all but one of the participants leave the room for a predetermined time. While all the others are absent, the remaining child hides a thimble, or other small object. Upon returning, the children hunt for the hidden object and the person who finds it is the next to hide it.

Appendix D: The Great September Gale

This tremendous hurricane occurred on the 23rd of September, 1815. I remember it well, being then seven years old. A full account of it was published, I think, in the records of the American Academy of Arts and Sciences. Some of my recollections are given in *The Seasons,* an article to be found in a book of mine entitled *Pages from an Old Volume of Life.*

I'm not a chicken; I have seen
Full many a chill September,
And though I was a youngster then,
That gale I well remember;
The day before, my kite-string snapped,
And I, my kite pursuing,
The wind whisked off my palm leaf hat;
For me two storms were brewing !

It came as quarrels sometimes do,
When married folks get clashing;
There was a heavy sigh or two,
Before the fire was flashing, ---
A little stir among the clouds,
Before they rent asunder, ---
A little rocking of the trees,
And then came on the thunder.

Lord ! how the ponds and rivers boiled !
They seemed like bursting craters !
And oaks lay scattered on the ground
As if they were p'taters ;
And all above was in a howl,
And all below a clatter, ---
The earth was like a frying-pan,
Or some such hissing matter.

It chanced to be our washing-day,
And all our things were drying ;
The storm came roaring through the lines,
And set them all a flying ;
I saw the shirts and petticoats
Go riding off like witches ;
I lost, ah ! bitterly I wept, ---
I lost my Sunday breeches !

I saw them straddling through the air,
Alas ! too late to win them ;
I saw them chase the clouds, as if
The devil had been in them ;
They were my darlings and my pride,
My boyhood's only riches, ---
"Farewell, farewell," I faintly cried, ---
"My breeches ! 0 my breeches !"

That night I saw them in my dreams,
How changed from what I knew them !
The dews had steeped their faded threads,
The winds had whistled through them !
I saw the wide and ghastly rents
Where demon claws had torn them ;
A hole was in their amplest part,
As if an imp had worn them.

I have had many happy years,
And tailors hind and clever,
But those young pantaloons have gone
Forever and forever !
And not till fate has cut the last
Of all my earthly stitches,
This aching heart shall cease to mourn
My loved, my long-lost breeches !

The Complete Poetical Works of Oliver Wendell Holmes, Cambridge Edition, Houghton, Mifflin and Co., NY,

Appendix E: Cape Cod Weather Events

Notations are from the *New England Weather Book* by David Ludlum. (Editorial changes by the author.)

1626 - Dec 17 - Storm which caused first recorded shipwreck on Cape Cod: *Sparrowhawk* was shipwrecked off Nauset.

1635 - Aug 15 (?) - Great hurricane; same punch as 1938 hurricane; 14 ft tide; this was the storm in which Anthony Thacher and his family were shipwrecked and all but he and his wife drowned.

1638 - Earthquake near Plymouth - estimated intensity of 9

1638 - Aug 13 - Storm - double tide in Mass Bay - described by Gov. Winthrop in Journal

1641 - Nov 22 -Great windstorm; as fierce as hurricane - John Winthrop

1645 - Nov 8 – Northeaster; 3 vessels beached

1675 - Sep 7 - 2nd colonial hurricane

1676 - Sep 30 - Ephraim Howe in boat blown off Cape Cod by storm - rescued off Nova Scotia by schooner; sons and 3 others died

1677 - Dec 14 - Severe storm – mentioned by Rev. John Cotton

1683 - Aug 23 - Hurricane up Connecticut River Valley

1697 -1698 - Winter - Severest of the century

1713 - Aug 30 - Hurricane hits New London

1717 - Feb 27 - March 7 - 4 storms, 2 major, 2 minor; 3 ft of snow in Boston

1717 - Apr 27 - Cape storm; *Widah* wrecked off of Eastham

1723 - Mar 6 - Exceedingly high tide - unequalled until 1851

1723 - Nov 10 - Hurricane

1727 - Sep 27 - Hurricane- shipping losses

1740 - 1741 - Winter - Severe periods in November, early January, and end of February; thought to be more severe than 1697 - 1698; Boston harbor froze for 30 days

1743 - Nov 3 - Great damage by hurricane - tides within 4" of 1723 level

REFLECTIONS OF CAPE COD

1747 – 1748 - Winter - 30 snowstorms between Dec 25 and April - snow more than 4' deep in Boston

1749 - Spring drought - April to early July

1749 - Oct 19 - Hurricane; 7 vessels ashore on Martha's Vineyard

1755 - Earthquake near Cape Ann; estimated intensity of 8

1759 - June 8 - June coastal storm - perhaps hurricane

1761 - Summer drought until mid-August

1761 - Oct 23 - Hurricane - severest in 30 years; great shipping losses

1762 - Summer drought returns until August 18

1770 - Oct 20 - A late season hurricane - A furious gale of wind was accompanied by a tidal wave which changed the whole east and south shores of the Cape. Sand hills as high as 60 feet were deposited in some lowlands and saltmarshes. It washed away a sand point off of Nauset and boats could no longer use the Boatmeadow Creek as a canal across the Cape at Orleans. In 1804, town residents dug it out and called it Jeremiah's Cutter. C. Townshend, "Notes on Early Chart of Long Island Sound and its Approaches", US Coast & Geodetic Survey Report, 1890, pp 775 - 777

1778 - Aug 12 - Hurricane; prevented battle between French and British fleets off RI; heavy coastal shipping damage

1778 - Nov 2 - 3 - Storm in which *HNIS Somerset* was grounded off Wellfleet and crew captured; *Somerset* grounded 6 p.m. on 2nd; 21 of 500 men drowned

1780 - Jan - Feb - Great freezeup, all harbors frozen; severest of 18th century

1780 - May 19 - Dark day - candles required at noon - caused by smoke from fires

1786 - Dec 4 - 5, 7 - 8, 9 - 10 - Three snowstorms; Kingston had 48" on ground

1802 - Feb 22 - Great Northeaster - three Salem Indiamen wrecked on Cape Cod

1804 - Oct 10 - Snow hurricane with very destructive winds

1806 - Aug 23 - Great hurricane struck Cape Cod - deluges ruined crops; shipping losses

1815 - Sep 23 - 10 a.m. - 2 p.m. - tide rose 8 feet higher than usual in the highest course of the tide, and the bay was several feet higher still. (Freeman, History of Cape Cod Vol. 1, pp 606-607) - This was Great September Gale - enormous shore damage - made famous by poem by Oliver Wendell Holmes. If the tide had been 15" higher, it would have swept over the Cape (Cape Cod Handbook of History. by CW Swift, 1902) (See Appendix D for *The September Gale*, by Oliver Wendell Holmes).

1816 - Year without a summer - a volcanic explosion near Java meant weather was overcast and cool

1819 - Nov 9 - Dark day - rainfall impregnated with burned leaves

1821 - Sep 3 - Hurricane with big storm tide (Redfield's hurricane)

1823 - March 30 - Great northeast snowstorm; Nantucket Barometer 28.83; 18" snow in Boston, 24" in Providence

1825 - June 4 - Hurricane which did great damage to shipping in New England harbors

1825 - June -Heat wave June 7 - 12 - above 90 all days, 96 in Boston June 11 & 12

1825 - July - Heat wave July 7 - 12 and 20 - 31; July 11 & 12 over 102

1829 - Feb 20 - Major snow and wind storm - at Providence, 18 - 24" snow and 10 ft drifts (Barnstable Journal Feb 23, 1829)

1830 - Summer - severe drought - used salt marsh hay to feed animals (Fawsett, Cape Cod Annals. p70)

1830 - Aug 29 - Strong Gale; schooner *President* driven ashore near Highland Light (Barnstable Patriot)

1831 - Jan 16 Great snowstorm swept entire Atlantic seaboard; Boston 24", New Bedford 36"

1831 - Storms in 1831 turned Great Island of Yarmouth into a promatory, rather than an island (These Fragile Outposts. by Chamberlain)

1834 - Dec 15 - Heavy gale from SSW with snow - schooner *Enterprise* came on shore at Sandy Neck Light - very cold - ice made fast the schooner,- lighthouse keeper's journal

1835 - Cold week in Early January 1835 - below zero - one night Providence – minus 26; January 6 extreme cold - "schooner stranded near the light" - Feb 8 - "harbor all shut up with ice" - Lighthouse keeper journal at Sandy Neck

1835 - Nov 11 - South West gales beached 8 ships on Cape Cod

1835 - Dec 16 - 17 - New England's bitterest daylight - temperature – minus 12 in Boston and 40 mile per hour wind from NW

1839 - End of January - Rainstorm; massive thaw

1839 - Dec 15 - First of triple storms of 1839 - gales swept Mass Bay - 50 Gloucester vessels wrecked in harbor

1839 - Dec 22 - Second of triple storms

1839 - Dec 28 - Third of triple storms - barometer 28.77 - 24 inches of snow in Hartford, CT

1841 - Oct 3 - A two day gale, unprecedented in its destruction, swept over the Cape. During the course of this storm, Mill Pond and Follins Pond became silted up to such a degree that their value as fishing grounds was thereafter just a memory. Many people of the village [Weir Village] chose to move after this disastrous event, taking their houses with them - (Yarmouth Historic Commission, *Yarmouth, Old Homes* p. 50); The tide which always had come with force up Chase Garden Creek never came again (YHC, *Yarmouth, An Historical Inventory* p. 63); Truro, Dennis, and Yarmouth lost 87 men in this storm (Morison, p. 311)

1846 - Storm -date unknown - much damage to fishing fleets

1849 - Oct 7 - Offshore hurricane brushed Cape Cod. Henry Thoreau described scene in *Cape Cod*

1851 - Apr 16 - Great tide with a gale highest tide in Boston since 1723

1851 Oct 1 - Yankee Gale - hit the mackerel fleet hard - several died in Dennis - This is believed to be the Minot Gale of 1851, where waters rose 18 feet in Barnstable "Years later [unknown date] during another storm, Cape Cod

Bay's water coursed over the great marshes and reached Barnstable's main highway [today is Route 6A] (p 257 *These Fragile Outposts* by Chamberlain)

1852 - Apr 6 - Severe gale and snowstorm - many vessels ashore. Clipper *Hippogriffe* launched the day before - *Yarmouth Register* April 15, 1852

1853 - Dec 29 Central Wharf nearly destroyed by severe Northeaster with snow. high winds and tide. The store and packing shed of Hawes and Taylor were washed away. Tide 8" higher than 1852 storm - *Yarmouth Register*. Dec 30, 1853

1856 - Winter - It was so bad that the lightship LV4 had to be withdrawn from Bishop and Clerks Ledge. A lighthouse was subsequently built.

1856 - Aug 21 - Tropical storm; heavy rain

1857 - Jan 18 - 19 - Northeaster followed by cold; Nantucket; minus 11 degrees Jan. 23

1857 - Feb 10 - Severe freshets - resulted from very warm February following a severe January'

1862 - Feb 23 - The Gale of 1862 - single most destructive storm ever to strike New England fishery - On Georges' Bank - 15 schooners and 120 men lost

1867 - Jan 17 - Severe gale and snow paralyzed northeast

1869 - Sept 8 - Great storm (hurricane) in Buzzards' Bay - much maritime damage and flooding

1873 - Aug 24 - Grand Banks hurricane; 1123 vessels wrecked

1874 - Apr 25 - It snowed every Saturday in April - *Yarmouth Register*

1875 - June 18 - Severe coastal storm along eastern seaboard

1879 - Aug 18 - 19 - Hurricane - landfall at Buzzards Bay - extensive shore damage

1879 - Oct 28 - Offshore hurricane; minor damage

1881 - Sep 6 - Famous yellow day; smoke filtered sun (forest fires in Michigan)

1885 - Sep 22 - Offshore hurricane - 35 miles East of Nantucket

1886 - Jan 9 - Blizzard of 1886

1888 - Nov 25 - 27 - Late season hurricane

1888 Mar 12 - Blizzard of 1888; mostly rain and slush on Cape Cod

1889 - Aug 3 - Tornado at Provincetown(?); if so, only tornado on Cape

1893 - Aug 21 - Hurricane to east; moderate gales and heavy rain; followed by 3 more hurricanes in western New England between Aug. and Oct.

1894 - Apr 12 Severe coastal storm

1896 - Aug 19 - Waterspout in Vineyard Sound - 3600 ft. high

1896 - Sep 10 - Hurricane crossed Martha's Vineyard

1896 - Oct 12 - 13 - Destructive easterly gales

1898 - Nov 28 - Portland storm - heavy snow and gale; Mill Bridge in Yarmouth Port washed away; Long Wharf carried away

1899 - Feb 12 - 14 - Great Eastern Blizzard - Woods Hole barometer 28.86"; blizzard followed severe cold wave the week before

1905 - A "four quilt winter" - Blizzard Jan 25, 1905 - 5 masted coal schooner *Harwood Palmer* grounded off Lone Tree Creek; 4 masted *Alice May Davenport* came ashore at Dennis - described in Feb 11, 1905 *Register*. Ice more than 8 ft thick rendering relief operations impossible - ice went out March 10th - *Davenport* floated free March 21; *Palmer* had problems - finally free May 20 - *Register* article Jan 6, 1977 M. Milliken

1909 - Dec 25 - Coastal storm; wind 72 mph at Hull; very high tide

1914 - Feb 12 - Provincetown at minus8 degrees; coldest since 1857

1916 - Jul 21 - Ex-hurricane crossed Martha's Vineyard - heavy rain for three days

1918 - Feb 5 - Coldest day on Nantucket; minus 6.2 degrees; winter was coldest of 20th Century

1920 - Dec 5 - 7 - 3" of ice in Boston fell on top of 16" of snow on ground

1924 - Aug 26 - Offshore hurricane center 50 miles from Nantucket; much rain

1933 - Sep 17 - Hurricane passed 75 miles SE of Nantucket - heavy rain

1934 - Feb - Coldest month since 1857 - minus 17 at Providence

1936 - Sep 19 - Hurricane 40 miles East of Cape Cod - Provincetown 7-3/4" rain

1938 - Sep 21 - Hurricane, 121 mph winds (winds on Cape 75 - 90 mph), 588 lives lost, unprepared - almost a century since a really big storm had hit area; direct wind damage on Cape was not the greatest threat, storm surge and accompanying storm waves were - high tide and storm surge coincided in Buzzard's Bay

1940 - Feb 14 - Gale force northeaster; hundreds stranded

1944 - Sep 14 - Hurricane - 100 mph winds, 31 deaths, high tide passed 3 hours before gales struck - Elms ripped out in Yarmouth Port; Cape suffered severely

1944 - Oct 21 - Second hurricane of 1944; 50 miles SE of Nantucket - storm surge and high tide did not coincide

1945 - Nov 29 - Severe northeaster; 40 mph winds in Boston for 24 hours

1947 - 48 - Snowiest winter in south New England

1950 - Sep 11 - 12 - Hurricane Dog 85 miles from Nantucket; surf damage

1952 - Feb 18 - Gale that sank *Pendleton* & *Fort Mercer* - both broke in half; 62 mph gusts; *Pendleton* crew saved by Coast Guard boat from Chatham

1952 - Feb 27 - Cape Blizzard, 18" of snow at Hyannis, 70 mph, 10,000 homes without power

1954 - Aug 31 - Hurricane Carol - almost a twin to 1938 hurricane - high tide and storm surge coincided

1954 - Sep 11 - Hurricane Edna, 100 mph winds; crossed Cape Cod

1954 - Oct 15 - Hurricane Hazel; mostly in NY

1955 - Aug 12 - 13 - Hurricane Connie; heavy rains

1955 - Aug 17 - 19 - Hurricane Diane; more heavy rains

1956 - July 25 - Fog - *Andrea Doria* hits *Stockholm*

1958 - Feb 16 - 17 - Northeast snowstorm; blizzard conditions

1960 - Sept - Hurricane Donna; 100 mph winds, tide did most damage

1960 - Dec 11 - 12 - Northeaster on Cape; blocked highways with snow; gale force wind, blizzard conditions

1961 - Feb 3 - Snowstorm, Nantucket more than 14"

1961 - 1966 - Severe drought in New England

1961 - Sep 21 -- 26 - Hurricane Esther did look off Block Island; rain but minimal damage

1962 - Aug 29 - Hurricane Alma 50 miles SE of Nantucket; some boat damage

1963 - Oct 29 - Hurricane Ginny 125 miles SE of Cape Cod, winds 65 mph on Nantucket

1964 - Sep 14 - Hurricane Dora well east of Cape Cod - heavy rain on 14th on Cape

1964 - Sep 23 - 24 - Hurricane Gladys - heavy rain on 24th

1966 - Jun 14 - Hurricane Alma moved over Cape Cod as a light to moderate rainstorm - no longer a hurricane

1967 - May 26 - 6.5"of rain on Nantucket

1969 - Feb 24 - 28 - Snow fell for 100 hours; Boston 26.3"

1969 - Sep 9 - Hurricane Gerda - passed over Nantucket Lightship 75 miles SE of Nantucket; Nantucket 40 mph; some rain

1971 - Mar 4 - Winter hurricane - 100 mph winds; Cape barometric pressure 28.5"

1971 - Sep 14 - Hurricane Heidi 60 miles east of Cape Cod

1972 - Sept 3 - Hurricane Carrie passed short distance east of Cape Cod; 100 mph wind; heavy rain; disrupted Labor Day travel

1975 - Aug 2 - Record hot day; 107 in New Bedford

1978 - Feb 12 (?) - Blizzard of 1978, tides more than 15 feet high in Boston, Outermost house washed away

1984 - Mar 29 - Eldia storm, classic northeaster with 80 - 90 mph winds

1987 - Jan 2 - Chatham North beach breached in storm (same breach shows in 1880 map of Chatham)

1991 - Aug 19 - Hurricane Bob

1991 - Oct 31 (?) - No name storm - also called the Perfect Storm, tide 14.3 feet high in Boston

1992 - Dec - Shore line takes battering, just above 13 ft flood at Boston

1996 - Hurricane Edouard - trees toppled on Cape; gridlock

2001 - Mar 6 - 7 - Blizzard of 2001, much hype, slow to develop, Plymouth Route 3A closed – 2 - 3 foot waves breaking over road and barrier beach, much beach erosion

References and Suggested Reading

Cemeteries

Chase, Theodore and Gabel, Laurel. *Gravestone Chronicles I*. New England Historic Genealogical Society, 1990.

Sloan, David Charles. "The Last Great Necessity." *Cemeteries In American History*. The John Hopkins University Press Ltd., London, 1991.

Blachowicz, James. "The Gravestone Carving Traditions of Plymouth and Cape Cod." *Markers XV*, (1998).

Military

Brake, Captain Fred E. Q.M.C. *Camp Edwards Is Completed.*

Private Interview With Mr. Basil Dandison, May 17, 2002.

Ryder, John J. "Reminiscences Of Three Years' Service In The Civil War. *By A Cape Cod Boy*, Reynolds Printing, New Bedford, Mass, 1928.

A Journey Towards Freedom, Mercy Otis Warren, http://library.thinkquest.org/10966/data/bwarren.shtml

Garraty, John A and Carnes, Mark C, eds. *American National Biography*, New York: Oxford University Press, 1999. Boatner, Mark Mayo III, *Encyclopedia of the American Revolution*. New York: David McKay Company, 1966.Bunker Hill Exhibit / Biography / James Warren, The Massachusetts Historical Society. (2000).http://www.masshist.org/bh/warrenbio.html

Mullett, C.F., ed., "Some Political Writings of James Otis" (1929). Biography by Tudor, W. (1823, repr. 1970). *Otis, James*. Encyclopedia.com 2002. Lycos, Inc. (2001). http://www.encyclopedia.com/html/o/otis-jam.asp.

Lossing, Benson J. "Our Country". *How did James Otis die?*, (1877).

http://www.publicbookshelf.org/public_html/Our_Country_vol_2/howdidja_cd.html

DOUGLASS: James Otis, "Against the Writs of Assistance," 1761, Orators of America (New York: G. P. Putnam's Sons, 1900) part 1, pp. 23, http://www.nhinet.org/ccs/docs/writs.htm

Otis, James, http://kids.infoplease.lycos.com/ce6/people/A0837052.html

The Showmaker Who Spied For The Revolution, http://www.capecodtravel.com/archive/apy_1099.shtml. (2002). eCape, Inc. & CapeCodTravel.Com.

Pickering, James H., Michigan State University. *Enoch Crosby, Secret Agent of the Neutral Ground: His Own Story,* Published in *New York History,* Vol. XLVII, No. 1 (January 1966), pp. 61-73. New York State Historical Association, (1966). http://webserver1.oneonta.edu/cooper/articles/nyhistory/19 66nyhistory-pickering.html

Jensen, Merrill. *The Founding of a Nation: A History of the American Revolution, 1763-1776. (1968).* Maier, Pauline. *From Resistance to Revolution: Colonial Radicals and the Development of Opposition to Britain 1765-1776,* (1972). Bushman, Richard L. *Revolution: Outbreak of the Conflict,* http://www.historychannnel.com/perl/print_book.pl?ID=356 31

Phillips, Michael. (1996). Maritime History Page. *CSS ALBEMARLE.* http://www.cronab.demon.co.uk/alb.htm

Ericsson, John, http://search.biography.com/print_record.pl?id=14599

COLONEL JOSEPH ELDRIDGE HAMBLIN, http://www.falmr.org/hambin.htm

Joseph Eldridge Hamblin, Virtual American Biographies, Appleton's 1886 Encyclopedia, Edited Appleton's Encyclopedia, 2001. Virtualology. http://famousamericans.net/josepheldridgehamblin/

Iacuessa, Mike, *U-boat attack!,* Cape Cod Times, November 10, 1991.

Johnson, Caleb. Massasoit. Mayflower Web Pages, 1998. http://members.aol.com/calebj/massasoit.html

Towns and Villages and Livelihood

Harmon, Anne N. *Ambergris And Arrowheads: Growing up on Cape Cod In the 1930s and 1940s.*

Brigham, Albert Perry. "Cape Cod And The Old Colony. G. P. Putnam's Sons, 1920.

Sheedy, Jack and Coogan, Jim. "Cape Cod Companion"*: The History and Mystery of Old Cape Cod.* Harvest Home Books in cooperation with *The Barnstable Patriot*, 1999.

King, Roger H. "Cape Cod and Plymouth Colony in the Seventeenth Century*."* University Press of America, Inc. (1994).

Kittredge, Henry C. "Cape Cod Its People and Their History." Houghton Mifflin Company, 1968.

Earle, Alice Morse. "Customs And Fashions In Old New England." Heritage Books, Inc., 1992.

Dos Passos, Katharine and Shay, Edith. "Down Cape Cod." Robert M. McBride & Company, 1947.

Neal, Allan. "Cape Cod *Is a Number of Things*." The Register Press, 1954.

Smith, John Braginton and Oliver, Duncan. "Port On The Bay." *Yarmouth's Maritime History on the 'North Sea' 1638 to the present.* Historical Society of Old Yarmouth. 2001.

Schneider, Paul. "The Enduring Shore." *A History Of Cape Cod, Martha's Vineyard, and Nantucket.* Henry Holt and Company, LLC, 2000.

Swift, Charles A. "History Of Old Yarmouth." The Historical Society Of Old Yarmouth, 1975.

Dodge, John W. *History – First Congregational Church Yarmouth.*

Canning For Patriotism. The Register, October 5, 1978.

Time And The Town – A Provincetown Chronicle, Mary Heaton Vorse.

Vuilleumier, Marion. "The Town Of Yarmouth, Massachusetts: A History, 1639-1989, The Historical Society Of Old Yarmouth, 1989.

Baker, Florence W. "Yesterday's Tide." Printed In The United States Of America, 1941.

Clipper Ship History. Clipper Financial, http://www.clipperfinancial.com/history.htm.

Transportation

Farson, Robert H. "Cape Cod Railroads." Cape Cod Historical Publications, 1993.

Farson, Robert H. "The Cape Cod Canal." Cape Cod Historical Publications, 1993.

Druett, Joan. "Hen Frigates." Simon & Schuster, Inc., 1999.

Clark, Admont Gulick. "Sea Stories Of Cape Cod and the Islands." Lower Cape Publishing, 2000.

Bray, Mary Matthews. *A Sea Trip In Clipper Ship Days*.

Weather

Emmet, Richard and Alan. *Storm Warnings*. Massachusetts Audubon Society, Sanctuary, November/December 1992.

Woodbridge, Kim A. *The Summer of 1816*. The HTML Writers Guild, 1996-2001.

Daub, Suzanne. *Winter Freeze-Ups*. YESTERDAY'S ISLAND, November-December 1990.

The Hero Of The Famous Portland Gale, The Cape Codder, Thursday, March 5, 1970.

Hendy Jr., Mrs. William R. *This Cold Snap Tough, But 1873 Was Tougher.* Cape Cod Standard Times, 1961.

Brett, Elise. *'Twas in 1778, a storm wrecked the frigate Somerset.* Sunday Cape Cod Times, November 19, 1978.

The Monomoy Disaster March, 1902, Search for Monomoy Disaster at http://www.capecodtravel.com/

INDEX

Record Your Reflections Here